30 DAYS
to SUCCESS
PLANNER & GUIDE

by POWERFUL WOMEN TODAY

CAROLINA M. BILLINGS

Published by PWT Press
3 Centre St. #202
Markham, ON L3P 3P9
Canada

Author Carolina M. Billings's email: publishing@powerfulwomentoday.com

Limits of Liability and Disclaimer of Warranty

Disclaimer

Copyright Use and Public Information

ISBN: 978-1-7771146-2-6

Table *of* Contents

Dedication

To all Women ready to break free from the past, ready to challenge-self and begin to author the best story of your life.

Introduction

by Carolina M. Billings

5 Reasons Why
30-DAY CHALLENGES
WILL CHANGE YOUR LIFE FOR GOOD

THE POWER OF 30-DAY CHALLENGES

If I were to pick one word as the catalyst to change is ***courage***. It takes courage to go outside your comfort zone and there's something about a challenge that triggers our competitive and playful instincts, which is incredibly useful when it comes to building new habits. Personally, I've experienced that 30-day challenges have been ***the key to successfully building strong new habits*** in my day-to-day life.

The day you wake up and say, "I want to change my life,"
is a special day. You've acknowledged something's missing.
You're ready to take action.

The easiest way to change is not through sudden abstinence or self-induced hardship. Sudden changes, *while going cold turkey may work for some, end up creating anxiety*, stress and should your will break, it can lead to self-judgement and negative self-talk.

The best way to introduce change in your life is to go towards something else. Forward motion. To transform your life, you must, in some ways, transform yourself. Our book shares with you are ten ways you can **change your habits and your mindset**.

Our authors share the stories of the moment they knew change had to be made. They also share strategies to slowly introduce new patterns, ideas and possibilities. The path to life transformation is long and winding. These practices will help you become the person you need to be to see it through.

Reason #1
IT TAKES AT LEAST 21-DAYS TO FORM A NEW HABIT

The primary reason why 30-day challenges are awesome when it comes to forming new habits (and making them stick) is that it takes *at least* 21 days to form a new habit. And since we're talking about 30-day challenges here, it means that we've covered those crucial initial 21 days of starting our new habit.

In fact, it means that when our challenge is completed, the new habit has had **enough time to be completely ingrained in our behaviour and the neural pathways of our brain**. A truly strong habit has been formed after these 30-days.

Unfortunately, research is still divided on this topic and there's no single specific timeframe that's shown to be the tipping point when it comes to making a habit truly internal in our system. However, the general view is that it takes *at least* 21 days to build a new habit successfully.

It's much harder to successfully go through the initial phase of 21 days when you don't have a clear goal or challenge set for yourself. Therefore, many people fail within the first week of starting their new habit, as they have to rely on willpower and discipline alone, which are limited resources.

However, when you have a clear endpoint in the form of a 30-day challenge, actually sticking with it and successfully completing every single day is much more likely! All because of the reasons that follow next.

Reason #2
CHALLENGES ARE FUN

As soon as we decide to form a challenge around building a new habit, we've made it into a game. And games are fun. Much more fun compared to just disciplining and forcing yourself every single day. The desire to complete our 'game' is what makes the whole process a lot more pleasurable and fun to continue with. Our playful and competitive instincts will start to kick in and we view the challenge as something we truly *want* to complete.

Personally, I believe the key to success in any endeavour — whether it's business, health or habits — is to make it **as fun as possible and to anchor it towards a new experience you wish to have in your life**. The more fun you'll have, the easier it'll be to put in the effort and overcome obstacles along the way.

Reason #3
A PSYCHOLOGICAL PULL TOWARDS COMPLETING A CHALLENGE

There are 2 main psychological reasons why challenges are awesome:

1. The Zeigarnik Effect
2. Dopamine Release

First of all, the **Zeigarnik Effect**, which has been discovered by the Russian psychologist Bluma Zeigarnik in the 1920's. If you're not familiar with the term, it's the psychological effect that suggests that not finishing a task (or a 30-day challenge) creates mental tension, which keeps it **at the forefront of our memory**. In other words, we'll be thinking about it A LOT because it's an active 'task' that hasn't been completed yet. The only thing that will relieve this tension? Closure brought on by **completion** of the task (or challenge in our case)

We tend to remember what we don't complete — and therefore we'll try much harder to actually complete it fully. This way, it doesn't have to be at the forefront of our mind anymore. In essence, we are using psychology to our advantage (as an extra motivator) to build a solid foundation for forming the new habit.

Second of all, **dopamine release**. Because each time you cross off a successful day of your 30-day challenge, dopamine is released by our brain. And essentially, dopamine is the 'reward' hormone that makes you feel good and motivated after doing a certain activity.

When we feel the effects of dopamine, we're eager to **repeat the actions** that resulted in the dopamine release in the first place (neuroscientists refer to this as self-directed learning.)

In other words, we'll feel a psychological pull towards completing the next day of our challenge because our brain anticipates that it'll feel good after completion of the habit activity, as new dopamine will be released.

Again, we are using psychology to our advantage in order to actually complete our 30-day challenge. How cool is that!

Reason #4
CHALLENGES MEASURE YOUR PROGRESS

It has been said that *'that what's measured will be improved' or 'what you measure, you manage'*, I believe this to be very true. When most people start a new habit, they forget to measure or track their progress. They have an abstract view of their success or failure rate, thereby tricking themselves into feeling either overly optimistic about their progress or feeling overly pessimistic. Both lead to the fact that the new habit doesn't have enough consistency behind it to make it an internal part of their behaviour.

Tip: Manage the pattern not the day.

When doing a 30-day challenge, however, your progress is very clearly measured. You can instantly see if you're on track or if you need to step it up and maybe even restart your challenge if necessary. This way, you get real data and feedback about your actions and this is what'll lead to actual improvement and making sure the habit will stick.

Reason #5
CHALLENGES ACTIVATE YOUR COMPETITIVE INSTINCTS

As humans, we all have a degree of competitiveness within us. Challenges are a sure way to get those instincts out and use them to our advantage of building a new habit.

When we've set a challenge for ourselves, we are more driven, motivated and determined to accomplish it. We don't want to embarrass ourselves or let ourselves down, and we especially don't want to lose face in front of others.

You'll notice that as soon as you've set a challenge for yourself (and especially when done with multiple different people), you'll feel more driven than before. Use this internal power to your advantage to complete the 30-day challenge, which forms a strong foundation for your new habit to fully develop in your internal system.

CHALLENGES HAVE A CLEAR START- AND END-POINT

Compare this to many people's new year's' resolutions, which have no endpoint at all. This is a sure way to failure. When you have no endpoint in sight, you don't make use of the Zeigarnik effect, as there is nothing to 'complete'.

"A goal without a deadline is just a wish"

Second of all, when there is no clear endpoint in sight, the **likelihood of giving up** is a LOT higher. When we have no endpoint to work towards, we're much more likely to quit after we've missed a few days of doing our habit activity. We feel frustrated and bad about ourselves and we simply go on with our lives as normal.

However, when we have a clear endpoint to work towards, we're much more motivated to continue and actually accomplish the 30 days, even if we missed one or two days. Giving up on our challenge is a much more conscious and painful decision than simply letting our 'wish' of building a new habit fade slowly away.

References

1. Denmark, Florence L. (2010). "Zeigarnik Effect". In Weiner, Irving B.; Craighead, W. Edward (eds.). *The Corsini Encyclopedia of Psychology* (4th ed.). John Wiley & Sons. pp. 1873–1874. doi:10.1002/9780470479216.corpsy0924. ISBN 9780470170236.
2. https://medium.com/personal-growth-lab/6-reasons-why-30-day-challenges-will-change-your-life-for-good-2d78d2dc5665

Foreword

I am beyond thrilled to have the opportunity to expand the Mission and Vision of Powerful Women Today to Champion and Empower Women's Emotional and Financial Independence.

As you can imagine, the 30 Day challenges our experts write about are the product of a decade long continuous formal and self-directed learning, documenting, testing, failing, reflecting and understanding. All this learning has been summarized onto 11 Challenges conceptually.

To say that these 30 Day Challenges and the steps to achieve them will take 30 minutes, 30 weeks or 30 years is to begin to understand that life is organic, on-going it may as well be 30 lifetimes.

This workbook version of "Awaken your Emotional and Financial Independence" includes questions and spaces to write your answers so you can take-action for your own writing, reflecting and to begin to create your blueprint to success. It includes, exercises and suggested further reading. It is about the journey as much as the destination.

The biggest takeaway from this book is the need to take ACTION. It is knowing that there is only one person who has the ability to direct your life. That person is YOU.

Powerful Women Today is a social impact global movement. The sisterhood is real for those willing to embrace it with an open heart. There are so many ways to join our movement and be part of the change that will take women to income parity, to emotional self-sustainability and self-reliance. Yours and as many women in the world.

Big Love.

Carolina M. Billings
Founder & CEO
Powerful Women Today™

Dedication

To Charlie, my reason, vision, purpose, and reward;

the love of my life, my everything

Carolina M. Billings

15 STEPS TO AWAKEN YOUR EMOTIONAL AND FINANCIAL INDEPENDENCE

Whether you choose to work on one specific area of your life, each area of focus does not exist in a vacuum. One of the biggest reasons we self-sabotage can simply be that we are trying to build one room in a house without considering how it fits within the whole design both structurally and holistically.

POWERFUL WOMEN TODAY'S
15 STEPS TO AWAKEN YOUR INNER POWER

The Three Cap Stones

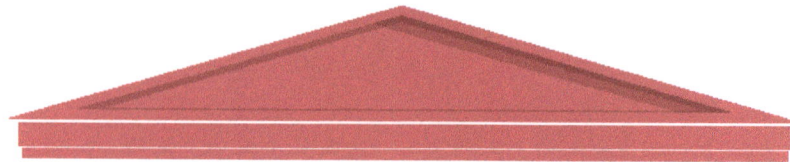

FULFILLMENT + TRANSCENDENCE + HAPPINESS

The Eight Pillars of Wellness & Success

PHYSICAL   SOCIAL   EMOTIONAL   OCCUPATIONAL   FINANCIAL   SPIRITUAL   INTELLECTUAL   ENVIRONMENTAL

The Four Foundations

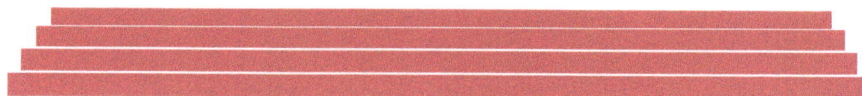

VISION + MISSION + PURPOSE + REWARD

The biggest myth in life is that we have time in the future.

The only time we have to be our best selves is now.

It's important to reflect deeply on the next set of questions, independent of outside context. Take the time you need to write down the answers to these questions.

1. Are you happy?

2. What are your goals?

3. How urgent are they?

4. What do you value? How do your goals align with what you value?

5. What does success look like? Do you know an example of someone who has achieved something similar to what you aspire to do?

6. What are your passions?

7. What is your life purpose?

8. What are you prepared to do to feel that you are the guiding force in your life?

9. What are you prepared to say no to?

10. What are you prepared to say yes to?

"Say yes and you'll figure it out afterwards."

Tina Fey

Why are we doing this on pen and paper?

A written goal brings clarity and focus. It gives you a direction. And by rewriting your goals you not only reaffirm what your goals are. You may also find new insights that bring more clarity and focus to your goal and life.

1. Writing things down helps you record everything that has your attention

2. Writing things down helps clear your mind

3. Writing things down helps clarify your goals, priorities, and intentions

4. Writing things down helps keep you motivated

5. Writing things down helps you recognize and process your emotions

6. Writing things down encourages daily progress

7. Writing things down enables a higher level of thinking, and therefore, more focused action

8. Writing things down develops your sense of gratitude

"When you write down your ideas you automatically focus your full attention on them. Few if any of us can write one thought and think another at the same time. Thus, a pencil and paper make excellent concentration tools."

One thing a lot of very successful self-improvement writers – Anthony Robbins, Brian Tracy, Zig Ziglar and so on – go on and on about is the importance of having written goals.

So, get comfortable, breath deep and let's get started.

This is your *Before*. Do not read ahead.

Paint me a picture.

On a scale from 1 to 10 tell us (you and me) honestly how do you feel?

How do I feel when	1	2	3	4	5	6	7	8	9	10
I wake up. Do I feel Happy?										
I look at myself in picture										
I put my clothes on										
The phone rings										
I check my emails										
I check my social media										
I visit my family										

How do I feel when	1	2	3	4	5	6	7	8	9	10
I get together with friends										
I tell people about my job										
I tell people about my dreams										
I check my bank account										
I open my bills										
I get into my car										
I think of God or Creator										
I pray/meditate/dream										
I think of love for self										
I think of love for others										
I feel loved										
I think of all that I am now										
I think of all I can be										
I think of all I can achieve										
I think how others see me										
I think how I see myself										
I think how I see my partner										
I think he/she sees me										

30 Day Challenge

PART I

The Four Foundations
VISION + PURPOSE + PLAN + REWARDS
WITHOUT THEM YOU WILL KEEP DOING THE SAME THING
EXPECTING A DIFFERENT RESULT

There are many ways to set goals and plans for the future. Some are sound strategies like SMART. It guides you to make sure your goals are Specific, Measurable, Attainable and Timely. These attributes for goal setting are valid. At least some of them. Absolutely goals should be specific but more often than not, time is not spent exploring and reflecting deep behind those goals. Knowing beyond what the final outcome you are wanting is as important as having the goal to begin with. I believe strategies like this keep you thinking small.

"If you don't like something, change it.
If you can't change it, change your attitude."
Maya Angelou

So, I ask you the most important questions

How ready am I to	1	2	3	4	5	6	7	8	9	10
Change										
Do whatever it takes										

Why?

WHAT ARE THE BIGGEST REASONS YOU FEEL

#RadicalChange is needed for **#RadicalResults**

Give me your top 5

1	
2	
3	
4	
5	

Use the available space to write up:

What is the worst thing that would happen if I do what is right for me?

What is the best thing that could happen if I do what is right for me?

What is the worst thing that would happen if I don't do what is right for me?

What is the best thing that could happen if I don't do what is right for me?

Conventional wisdom tells you that to make sure your goals are clear and reachable, each one should be:

☐ Specific (simple, sensible, significant).

☐ Measurable (meaningful, motivating).

☐ Achievable (agreed, attainable).

☐ Relevant (reasonable, realistic and resourced, results-based).

☐ Time bound (time-based, time limited, time/cost limited, timely, time-sensitive).

The problem with these is that it uses past knowledge which is limited knowledge.

Your goals and dreams should be so big that if they were to come true today you would poop your pants.

They should scare the living daylights out of you.

Why would someone want to live like that? Scared that if their dreams would come true they would not know what to do. That my Darling is exactly the point.

I do agree your goals should be Measurable otherwise how would you know you have attained them. They should also be Meaningful and Motivating. Agreed.

Under Relevant it insists on using *think small* concepts. Reasonable and realistic are limited by what society may have taught you. What others have expected of you and what you may have allowed yourself to think. My wish is for you to THINK BIG. To want big things for yourself even if reality right now is telling you otherwise.

You need to be able to see beyond your current circumstances.

"Doubt is a killer. You just have to know who you are and what you stand for."

PART II

The Eight Pillars of Wellness and Success
EMOTIONAL+ENVIRONMENTAL+FINANCIAL+INTELLECTUAL +OCCUPATIONAL+PHYSICAL+SOCIAL+SPIRITUAL

PHYSICAL SOCIAL EMOTIONAL OCCUPATIONAL FINANCIAL SPIRITUAL INTELLECTUAL ENVIRONMENTAL

YES, WE CAN HAVE IT ALL

We discussed the four foundations to awaken your emotional and financial independence. This is the groundwork and it's literally the foundation for creating your new reality.

When we think of success and goals, it isn't uncommon for us to compartmentalize. For example, our goal may be to lose weight or make more money.

However, even though it's easy to allocate a goal to a specific area of our lives (for example, in terms of money, we may think of career or business), the reality is that every single goal or pursuit affects every area of our lives.

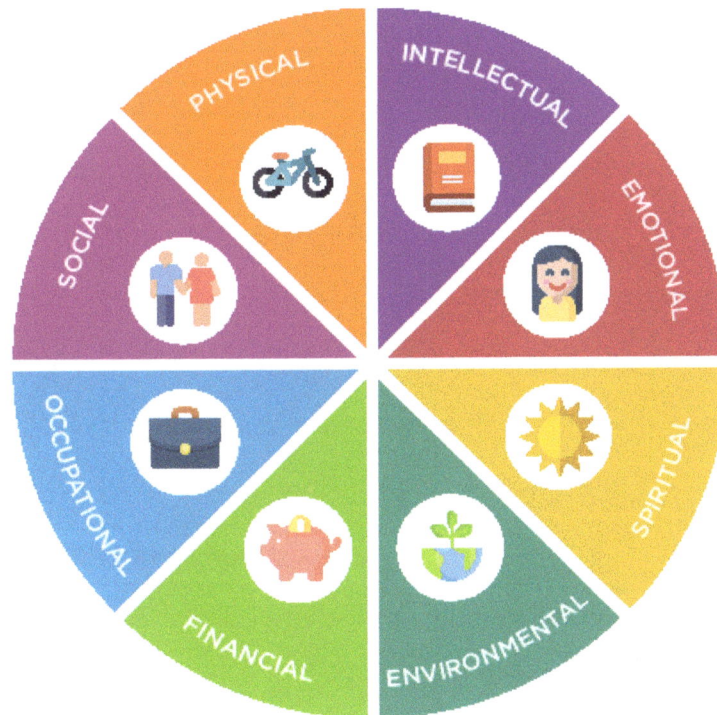

The eight-dimension model[1] was first identified in the 1960s as a theory illustrating the idea that all eight dimensions are interconnected.

This theory wasn't fully appreciated and embraced until the Wellness and Mental Health movements of the turn of the century, when mental health was recognized as a daily factor in everyday life and not something reserved for clinical last-hope interventions.

In 1995, Dr. Margaret Swarbrick began to correlate and integrate all eight dimensions during mental health psychiatric rehabilitation research, later published in the Psychiatric Rehabilitation Journal in 2006[2].

In this research, Dr. Swarbrick explains that a holistic approach is needed to truly experience the lasting effects of trauma.

There is a significant paradigm in the field of public mental health practice that encompasses a wellness approach. Her research presented a holistic wellness approach by comparing it to the existing traditional medical model of isolating and treating symptoms without examining the root of the problem that may originate or cascade into different dimensions of one's personal life.

Instead of viewing human needs in a stacking scaffolding format like Maslow's hierarchy of human needs (proposed in his 1943 paper, "A Theory of Human Motivation" in *Psychological Review*)[4], in which only once a need is satisfied can a personal focus on the next immediate aspirational aspect of their lives each representing a smaller segment than the one below, a holistic approach understands that a need and its effects can occur and manifest themselves simultaneously across all aspects of your life—thus, the term "holistic." – Dr. Swarbrick

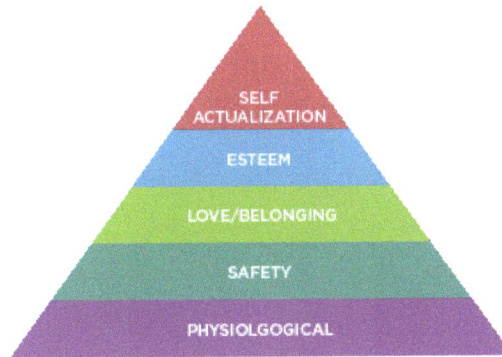

Consider this: When we feel financially stressed (e.g., increasing debt), we experience emotional stress (anxiety), sometimes leading to physical problems (illness), less effectiveness at work (occupational), and perhaps even questioning our own meaning and purpose in life (spiritual).

When we aren't working (occupational), we lose some of our opportunities to interact with others (social), can't get the quality foods and medical care we need to stay well (physical), and may need to move to a place that feels less safe and secure (environmental).

I have had clients come to me because they were extremely dissatisfied with their jobs and wanted a mentorship to change careers.

In the process of doing a deep dive into the root causes, it would surface that it was the client's personal relationship and the frustration she was experiencing at home that were causing her to hyper-focus on her career – which she unconsciously felt was something she could control, unlike her relationship with her partner, which at the time she felt hopeless about.

Stress, addiction, trauma, disappointment, and loss can impact our mental health, our emotional wellness, and the balance in our lives.

"You're going to be happy" said life,
"but first I'll make you strong."
Unknown

DOES HAVING IT ALL MEAN DOING IT ALL?

Success without fulfillment and happiness is the ultimate failure. Therefore, wellness and success are mutually inclusive aspects of awakening and experiencing your best self and creating your optimal life.

Wellness requires that we balance work with play and rest, that we balance time off for recuperation and recovery with living our lives fully and productively, and that we balance the desire for rapid change with the known effectiveness of slow changes to build good habits.[3]

The Eight Pillars for Wellness and Success are: (Notice how they are never listed in the same order, that is because they are circular, no beginning no ending)

- **Emotional**—Coping effectively with life and creating satisfying relationships.
- **Environmental**—Maintaining good health by occupying pleasant, stimulating environments that support well-being.
- **Financial**—Being satisfied with current and future financial situations.
- **Intellectual**—Recognizing creative abilities and finding ways to expand knowledge and skills.
- **Occupational**—Finding personal satisfaction and enrichment in one's work.

- **Physical**—Recognizing the need for physical activity, healthy foods, and sleep.

- **Social**—Developing a sense of connection, a sense of belonging, and a well-developed support system.

- **Spiritual**—Expanding a sense of purpose and meaning in life.

Awakening your emotional and financial independence is heavily reliant on identifying *how* your **Vision+Purpose+Plan+Rewards** fits into your future as well as being able to determine *what* your starting point is, and to integrate and execute the plan within the eight pillars of wellness and success.

Not only will doing this enable you to achieve a specific goal in one area of your life but you'll be able to see how this one goal will fit into all the areas of your life. A change in one will affect all, given that the composite of all is you — your life experience.

YES, YOU CAN HAVE IT ALL. THAT IS, *YOUR* ALL.

Reflection: Visualization of yourself being happy is somewhat different than visualizations of more physical things (like your dream home, or money visualization, for example). It's used, of course, to manifest happiness in your life, but it's a fantastic exercise for learning how to attract that feeling even in the stressful situations, when you're not feeling very satisfied with yourself or with your circumstances (you can read about how to "anchor" your feeling or state of mind in order to bring it back in whatever situation you need it).

Feeling happy will always help you in manifesting, because it's a positive emotion that adds to the strength of your thoughts, and helps relieving them of any negative connotation that may be hiding somewhere in your subconscious. That's why you can practice visualizing yourself being happy every time you're about to do some other visualization, as a preparation stage.

30 Day Challenge in Action

Self-awareness is the first step toward transformation. The Wheel of Life is a tool often used by mentors and coaches to be able to take a snap shot. A way for a client to check into their current state. It is quite simple, plot from 1 to 10, ten being the highest of best, as to where you are currently at. The image on the right is an example of one completed.

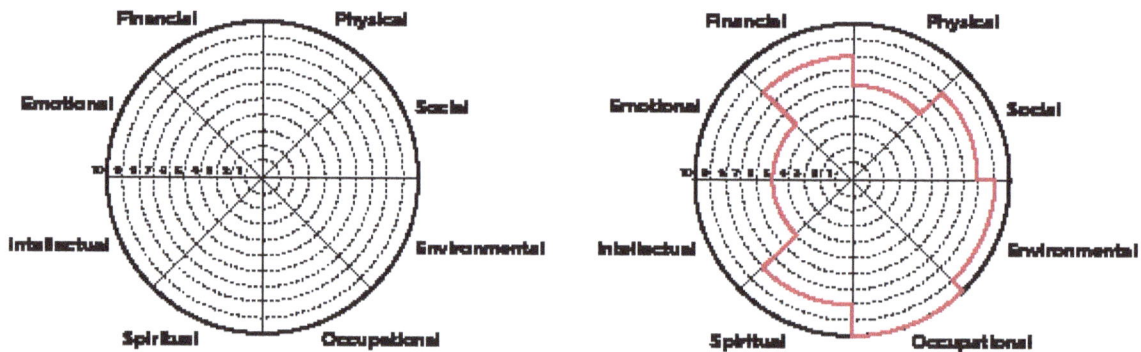

As simple it may appear, this is a great tool to examine what may be the road block. For example, someone that is feeling burned out may see their emotional wedge rated at a 5 of 10 such as in the example enclosed. If you notice, the occupational wedge is rated at a 10 of 10. This is most likely associated if you are spending all your energy on one wedge or area of your life, it is virtually impossible for it not to affect the others. What is amazing in this exercise is that, the snap shot is so fluid you could do a check in in the morning and depending what transpired during the day your wheel may look completely different.

It is not unusual for a client I am consulting with 1:1 to come to me because they feel the need to change jobs and want a transition strategy.

When we begin plotting on the wheel it may become clear that other areas of her life are being affected. Perhaps the intellectual wedge doing a deep dive surfaces as the real point of pressure. It could be that it is not the job per se, meaning the company or the industry even the job. Perhaps it is not being challenged or feeling that you are not being given the opportunity to apply all your potential. So, instead of giving up on all the good will and seniority, we begin to put together a strategy to do a pitch for career advancement or an expansion of duties.

What becomes powerful is not so much the plotting. That is the first step. What really brings about goal achievement is the action forward. Taking charge of your destiny is one of the most amazing byproducts of empowerment.

HOW DOES THE WHEEL WORK?

It is recommended that you work with a coach or mentor at least for a few sessions to get started. I have created webinars to walk you through it if you wish to tackle it on your own.   Let's say you plot spirituality at 3 of 10 and you have identified this is an area that you wish to develop. The question then becomes: What would make it a 4 out of 10. You then set up your goals for the week/ month or set period.

The secret to success is that the answers come from you. Not been pre-scribed on given to you with good intention by anyone else. In the example above, perhaps your answer will be to make a point to visit different places where spirituality is practiced so you find the one that resonates with you. You and your coach determine a reasonable time to check again after you have taken action towards your goal. At the next check in, you rate it again say now it has increased from a 4 out of 10. The question becomes what would make it a 5 out of 10.

Sometimes the wedge or area that gets identified as an area you are want-ing to work on is a bit more complex or there is a need for a deeper dive. Each wedge becomes its own wheel. For example, with Spirituality working together you may identify which areas of Spirituality you are wanting to explore.

Example
TAKING A DEEP DIVE ON SPIRITUALITY

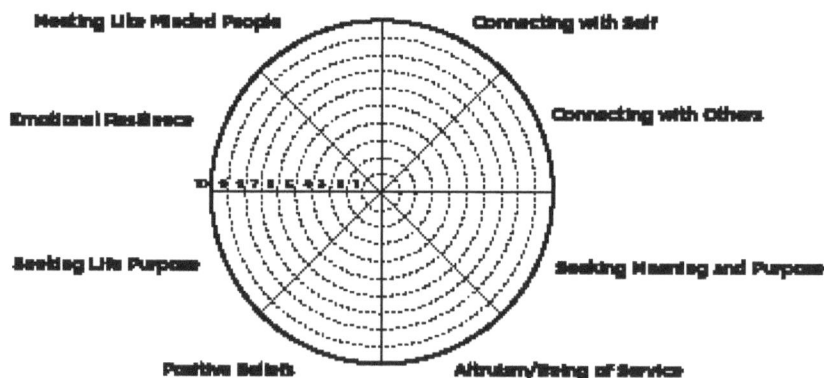

Remember it is extremely important that YOU help identify the categories for the wedges. We are trying to get to the bottom of your vision and purpose. There are no right or wrong answers. Visit our academy for more deep dive examples for each of the pillars.

About the Author

Carolina Billings, PhD (C), MA-IS, CHRL, SHRP-SCP, CPCC is a social impact entrepreneur with 15+ year's leadership experience in the fields of Business Development, Leadership, Branding, Human Resources and Finance.

Carolina is the founder of Powerful Women Today a boutique accelerator for success. A forum for the empowerment and optimization of women's status and lives.

Her sold out conferences, publications, social impact, and Diversity, Inclusion & Equity initiatives have received the continued support and accolades of key champions of women in business. Carolina is proud to call herself an advocate working wholeheartedly for the emotional and financial independence and prosperity of women and their dependents.

Her Boutique Management Consulting Firm is comprised of elite experts championing women's growth. Her ***#1MillionWomenChallenge*** aims at positively impacting 1 Million Women every year to bring awareness to end violence against women and strengthen mental health and end financial dependency.

She is a leader with global impact who Champions and Empowers Women's Emotional and Financial Independence. She is proud of her adoptive home in Canada as is proud of her Hispanic heritage.   She is a highly active advocate and champion of Social Justice, Diversity, Inclusion and Equity.

Carolina's dream is for every woman and little girl to realize that their uniqueness is their beauty and their talents their magic to love, touch lives, inspire others and shine brightest always.

Photo credit: Pheasant Lane Photography

Contact information
Carolina M. Billings, PhD (C), MA-IS, CHRL, SHRM-SCP, CWEC, CPCC, PCC
Company: Powerful Women Today
Email: carolina@powerfulwomentoday.com
LinkedIn: www.linkedin.com/in/carolinabillings
Facebook: www.facebook.com/bewhatnow
Website: www.powerfulwomentoday.com

Dedication

To all Who seek Holistic Balance In their Life

Dr. Linda Potts

To better understand why I do what I do, I would like to share my story. I was truly fortunate to be raised in an extremely healthy environment. We ate healthy consistently. My mom made everything from scratch, except bread, and we had exceptionally low sugar consumption, except for the fruit we ate. If we had a soda twice a month, that was a lot for us. We were never allowed to have caffeine. I was also raised vegetarian. We worked hard and played hard. I was also very athletic as a child and into my 40's.

When I was 11 years old, we moved to Thailand. It was an incredible experience, and I am very grateful to have had the opportunity to live in a foreign country. We lived there until I was 14 years old. One of the things we did there was volunteer at the Bangkok Adventist Hospital. One of the great things for me was there was a School of Nursing attached to the hospital compound and I became exceptionally good friends with many of the nursing students. Even though there was a significant age difference, it didn't seem to matter. With that experience, I became interested in becoming a Registered Nurse. Which I did. I received my Bachelor's in Nursing and passed the Boards to become a registered nurse. Most of my clinical experience was Emergency Room/Trauma, which I absolutely loved! I also had a variety of management positions throughout my years of practice, but my passion was always ER/Trauma. During that time, I was also a personal trainer and a natural bodybuilder, as well as a runner and a swimmer. I loved all of it. I was in excellent health consistently until the age of 42.

Super Bowl Sunday 1998 is the day my life changed forever. The day started out filled with joy and delight as I prepared food for the Super Bowl event at my home. Then in the afternoon, I suddenly fell to the floor and I could not get up due to severe right-sided abdominal pain. I told my date (now my husband), "If I did not know any better, I would think I was having a gallbladder attack." He offered to take me to the emergency room, but I said "No". As I said earlier, I was an ER/Trauma Nurse so I knew unless you have some type of major trauma, you can sit in the waiting room for an exceptionally long time. I told him I had to go to work the next day anyway so I would make sure I saw one of the doctors in the ER then. I did just that and of course they ordered a gamut of tests and x-rays. I was sitting in the waiting room in a wheelchair when the radiologist came out, who was a friend of mine, and said, "Linda, number one, I do not know how you are able to be sitting here and number two, every organ in your body is totally inflamed and we have no idea why!" That was the start of an exceedingly long journey for me. At that time, I was a single Mom with 2 young children, working 45 minutes from home, with a management position requiring my working 60-70 hours a week.

I was in and out of consciousness for 3 weeks. I gradually recovered somewhat from the acute situation but continued to have significant issues. I was in considerable pain most of the time, experienced extreme fatigue periodically, along with difficulty concentrating and focusing.

During the first two years of having these issues, I was working on completing my MBA. Occasionally, after walking across campus and up two flights of stairs for classes, the fatigue would be so bad I would have to lie down on one of the benches at the top of the stairs. It was during one of these events that my professor who was working with me for my thesis walked out of his office and saw me lying there. He immediately approached me and, concerned, asked if I was ok and if there was something he could do. I was embarrassed because I tried to hide my health issues the best I could from others finding out, especially my professors. I shared with him my story and the fact that none of the medical doctors I had seen had any idea what was going on with me. He was very compassionate and knowing I was to present my thesis before a panel the following week and knowing how stressful that can be, told me to just come to his office the following week when I felt better, sit and present my thesis just to him. That was a huge relief for me. I did just that and completed my MBA the Spring of 2000.

My health continued to deteriorate, despite the various medications and therapies prescribed for me. Eventually I was unable to carry on a conversation with anyone and have someone understand what I was trying to convey because my words were so garbled. I went to a variety of doctors who all seemed to be very baffled and unable to determine exactly what was going on with me. After 4 years of seeing multiple specialists, having a battery of tests, along with a variety of prescription medications which did not work, I was finally given the diagnosis of Lyme disease, fibromyalgia, and chronic fatigue syndrome. During that whole period, a lot of neurological damage had occurred, along with extreme fatigue and severe pain. I do not recall much of anything during those four years. By then I had to quit working and I had become bedridden due to the severity of the pain and extreme fatigue. My husband had to help feed me and get me to the bathroom. It was a very humbling experience for one being so independent my whole life.

My family doctor said, "Linda, you may have to live like this the rest of your life. I have done everything I know to do to help you." My immediate response to him was, "That is not an option!" It was with that knowledge, I decided to turn to Natural Medicine to see if there were solutions in that arena for me. The first natural health practitioner I saw was an acupuncturist. At that time, I was having trouble breathing, along with constant severe pain and extreme fatigue. I had had all the pulmonary function tests done, all normal and my pulse ox was "better than most people your age," so I was told. It didn't change the fact that I felt like I couldn't breathe well enough to get enough oxygen." During my first session, I learned that Chinese medicine had identified specific emotions directly related to different organs in the body. The acupuncturist asked me if I had had a recent loss of someone close to me to which I responded "Yes, my sister died." He said, "The lungs are affiliated with sadness and grief, which is why you can't breathe well." He was able to "open up" my lungs so I could take a deep breath again, all the way down to the base of my lungs. This was an exciting beginning to improving my health and learning about Nature Medicine. Although acupuncture was helpful, it was not sustaining. So along with that modality, I started experiencing a variety of natural health modalities, such as chiropractic, massage, far infrared sauna, ion cleanse foot bath, and cranial/sacral therapy.

One of the things that happened to me when people heard I was interested in trying natural medicine is suggestions of a borage of supplements that would surely cure whatever was ailing me. When a particular supplement would be recommended, it seemed to be presented as a miracle cure such as "My Aunt couldn't walk and now she can walk on water!"

None of them worked for me. Not even one! Nothing was addressing the root cause of my illness. I was extremely disappointed because my hopes were dashed over and over again. I was almost ready to give up with Natural Medicine when a friend from church recommended I go and have a particular type of screening done. It was all very foreign to me, but I said I would try it. During the screening, I was so intrigued. It was amazing what it found, yet I had no idea how it did it. One of the things it found first was parasites. Not Lyme but parasites. (Lyme did not show up on this initial screening but did in a subsequent screening.) Fascinating! I asked what type of parasites and the practitioner said it was parasites from the Philippines and then asked, "Does that make sense to you?" I said, "Yes, I lived in Thailand when I was a kid and we visited Philippines for two weeks on a vacation." Wow! I had had these in my body for 29 years and never exhibited symptoms prior.

I knew then this type of modality was going to help heal me and this was something I definitely needed to learn about.

It took six weeks for me to feel any improvement in my body because of the extreme pain I had been experiencing. But as the pain diminished, I noticed I no longer had Irritable Bowel Syndrome, my mental capacity had improved significantly, I finally slept 5 hours in a row and my energy level was improving. This was it. My pathway to healing.

I went on to become certified in bioenergetics so I, too, could do the type of screening I had received. Later I completed a master's in bioenergetics. I also got my doctorate in clinical religious counseling and doctorate in naturopathy and I am a Board-Certified Doctor of Natural Medicine. I have continued to maintain my RN License as well.

I opened my own practice in 2004 and opened my own Center, Healing Waters Wellness Center, in 2006.

I absolutely love what I do!

WHAT PROBLEM DO YOU WISH TO SOLVE IN THE WORLD?

I have a strong desire to help people understand that you can blend Eastern and Western Medicine and get great long-lasting results in obtaining and maintaining good health. It does not have to be either Western Medicine or Eastern Medicine. Blending the two methods can work, utilizing each of their strengths and supporting their weaknesses. Eastern medicine is not voodoo medicine. It

IS scientifically proven, contrary to what we have been led to believe. I believe in the validity of Western Medicine in multiple situations. In the United States, we have the best Emergency Care System. I tell my people frequently, "If I have an emergency do not take me to my Center, take me to an Emergency Room, preferably one with a Trauma Center."

Eastern medicine is great for preventative care and chronic issues. Western Medicine is not necessarily designed for those arenas. When I began my private practice, I visited several of the doctors I had gotten to know well from working in the emergency room to let them know what I was doing. They were open to hearing what I had to say since they knew me, and some said they were so glad I was doing what I do because they have so many patients that have chronic issues and they did not know what else to do for them. Some referred many patients to me.

In Western Medicine, we typically only deal with the physical. When utilizing Western Medicine, we feel if we mention anything related to emotional or mental concerns, people will think we have psychiatric issues and we will be referred to a therapist or psychiatric unit. However, in Natural Medicine, coming from a holistic perspective, we look at the physical, mental, emotional, and spiritual aspects of an individual. If one of these is out of balance it can cause any one of the others to become out of balance. When I speak of the emotional and mental aspects, I am referring to just the normal human emotions and ways we think. For the spiritual aspect we are referring to one's soul or spiritual journey, not necessarily about what religion you are or not affiliated with.

It is important to understand we are a whole person, and we need to examine all aspects of ourselves.

Typically, people come to me when they have tried all the Western Medicine avenues related to their specific health issue or concern and nothing has been resolved. When they come to me, I typically find there is an emotional, mental, or spiritual component that is out of balance because only the physical was addressed without resolution or healing occurring. Without the other aspects being addressed and resolved, the physical issue will typically continue.

WHAT DRIVES YOUR PASSION FOR IT?

I absolutely love what I do. Everybody around me can see and feel that. My Dad said to me one morning when I was over at his home to visit prior to my going to my Center, "I always like seeing you in the morning because I know you are going to have a good day." I was surprised and did not understand what he was referring to. I asked for an explanation and he said, "Because you love what you do, it's always a good day!"

I love being able to have an impact on someone's health. Seeing people feel better physically, happier, more stable emotionally, mentally clearer and spiritually lifted. I have the pleasure and joy of seeing people transform right in front of my eyes. What is better than that? It's such an awesome experience!

HOW IS YOUR METHOD/APPROACH DIFFERENT?

I look at my patients from a holistic perspective. So, I look to discover what is the root cause of the imbalance/s my patient is exhibiting or has been dealing with.

In Western Medicine we tend to look at the symptoms and give medication to block those symptoms or change those symptoms in a way that the patient no longer experiences them.

From the holistic health perspective, we work on finding what the root cause is so that the area can heal and then the symptoms will go away. We provide the support needed, such as supplements to support the body while healing or detoxing, and using other modes to help support the body while healing, and find balance so it can manage on its own.
I educate my patients about everything I do while working with them, why I am doing it, what I recommend and why I recommend it.

I educate my patients on paying attention to their thoughts. What are they thinking about related to themselves or others? Are they constantly thinking negative thoughts about themselves or others? Why? I help them recognize how what they think impacts their health, be it good or bad. It is important to be aware of our self-talk!

I educate my patients on focusing on themselves first and taking responsibility for what is going on in their life and their health. Too often, we tend to look at what is wrong with the people around us that upsets us rather than taking responsibility for our own self first. Stop being a victim and take control of your life. Learn to look at situations from a different perspective. When one's energy or vibrations shift and change, other people in one's life will shift and change, or they can just vibrate out of your life if it is not right for you anymore.

I teach my patients how to eventually manage their own health. I educate them on paying attention to what their body is trying to tell them. Our bodies are speaking to us all the time. It lets us know if everything is going great by having good health, happy, content moods, good brain health and being able to have a good night's sleep. If we are having symptoms that are not good, it is letting us know we need to pay attention and do something about it. We need to determine what is causing the symptom/s and resolve it as quickly as possible.

I educate my patients to note their symptoms and determine if it is due to an emotional imbalance, a mental imbalance, a spiritual imbalance or just a physical imbalance. If we only address the physical, we could be missing an important piece and never regain our total health.

Also, I educate my patients to pay attention to where in the body the symptom/s is located. Also, what time of day or night does that symptom appear? And what is going on in their life at the time the symptoms appear or just before. This information is immensely helpful to determine what aspect of their health is really the culprit for the symptoms and then know how to address them so they will be resolved.

The sooner we learn to pick up on what is out of balance, the easier it is to resolve it and get back to having good health, allowing us to function the way we want to and should be.

If one learns to read and know their own body, they will be able to know what is needed and utilize the resources available to resolve the issue.

I want people to become their own practitioner and know what is best for them at any given time. If they need further assistance, then they can come back to me for more guidance and support.

Typically, when our bodies get back into balance, we do not need to continue taking a lot of supplements on a consistent basis. Depending on how we eat, what we eat, sometimes when we eat, will determine if we need to take some form of vitamins and minerals. How we manage our emotions and the way we think - will dictate if we need to have support of some kind. Some natural practitioners believe one must always take a multivitamin or other form of supplement. I am currently not of that belief. From my perspective, it depends on the individual. Sometimes, you may not need to take something consistently but only occasionally when something goes off track. We are all unique and therefore, our needs may be different than someone else's. Pay attention to what your body is telling you.

I create guided and personalized pathways to provide optimal health, using proven philosophies and lasting results.

HOW HAS THIS METHOD CHANGED YOUR LIFE?

I got my life back! I was bedridden. I could not hold a job. I could not think straight. My neurological system was so damaged I could not carry on a conversation. I was in so much pain it was difficult to even move. There was a lot of damage done over a long period of time, so I am currently not able to do the full borage of what I was able to do prior to my collapse in 1998. I used to go on 10-day back-packing trips, paddle for days on lakes and rivers, portage our 2-person ocean kayak long distances through thick woods and over beaver dams. Ride my bike for 25+ miles without tiring, weight-train consistently 4-5 days a week, run 3-5 miles a day 3-4 times per week, rock climb, white water rafting, take long hikes, etc. And work full-time, raising 2 kids.

However, I am up and about. I have run my own business now for 16+ years. I can do day-hikes, ride a bike for several miles without having ramifications the next day. I can do yoga, pilates and other forms of workouts along with some resistive training. I can kayak/canoe with someone else. I garden and can clean my home. I still must be careful not to overdo it. People who do not know my health history would not be able to tell I used to be bedridden and unable to function doing everyday types of things.

WHAT CAN SOMEONE EXPECT?

I require each of my patients to complete an initial extensive history, so I know what is going on with them, detailing specific symptoms, what daily life is like, what foods they typically eat, how long they have had symptoms, what level of discomfort/pain they are currently having, what they have done to resolve their symptoms, what medications and/or supplements they have tried along with what were the results and what are they currently taking? Also, I want to know what foods they eat and how their digestive system is working. Also, how well their brain is functioning.

You are working with someone who understands what it is like to have poor health and nothing you have tried has worked until now. I will work right alongside you to educate you so you understand better what is going on with you and what your body is trying to communicate to you, and then what you can do to make the necessary changes to improve your health.

HOW IS YOUR METHOD/APPROACH DIFFERENT?

One of the major differences between Western medicine and natural medicine is that with natural medicine, it is a process. We are used to getting almost instant results or relief working with Western medicine but without resolution to the problem causing the symptoms, unless surgery is required. We take a prescription medication or an over-the-counter medication and the symptoms typically go away. Such as, you have a headache, you take Tylenol and in 20 minutes the headache is gone. The big difference is with Western medicine we deal only with the symptoms, whereas in natural medicine we work on finding the root cause and then work on healing that issue. So, it is a process, and most people are not used to it taking time for symptoms to resolve. With Western medicine if you stop taking the prescription medication, the symptoms typically will come back and sometimes the main issue or root cause will be worse. However, with natural medicine, finding and addressing the root cause, you take supplements for a period of time to allow healing to occur, and when you are without symptoms and stop taking the supplements the symptoms do not return (unless you return to the behaviors that caused the issue to begin with) and you feel better.

HOW WILL SOMEONE KNOW THEY HAVE SUCCEEDED AT THE FIRST 30 DAYS?

During my Initial consultation, I ask a lot of questions to determine what is going on with the patient. I ask what their biggest issue or concern is for coming to this appointment. Besides asking what their physical symptoms are, I also ask questions regarding their stress level, energy level, sleeping pattern, digestive issues, how much water they drink, as well as other pertinent questions, seeking for information to determine what other aspects of them may be out of balance besides the physical. I observe their body and listen to their responses, questioning if there is an emotional component? Is there a mental component, the way they think? Is there a spiritual component? I also utilize a sophisticated software program using biofeedback technology to assist with analyzing the input and create visual reports for the patient to see what their body is trying to reveal. During this screening I look at what may be out of balance with their organs, their glands, and systems. I also do a scan looking through the lens of an acupuncturist, seeing what meridians may be out of balance. I run a scan looking at their vertebrae to see what may be out of balance because all the vertebrae are energetically connected to all the organs. I look at the teeth because the teeth are energetically connected to all parts of the body. I also look at their energy centers or chakras as well as utilizing the law of five elements to examine what are the potential emotions that may be out of balance. I look at all that information collectively to determine what course of action needs to be taken and what education is necessary for the patient at that time. I will then make recommendations for supplements, such as homeopathic remedies, glandular support, herbal combinations, detoxing processes, and flower essences, which help with the emotional and mental aspects of an individual and at times the spiritual as well. I also may make recommendations for other types of modalities to help their bodies heal quicker. I request an update 3 days following our initial consultation and then again in a week. If there are any issues in between the initial appointment and the follow up appointment, I request they let me know. By 30 days, the patient will notice multiple symptoms have either decreased or no longer exist. It depends on the length of time each patient has had symptoms; how strong their immune system is and how willing they are to do their part in their healing process. It must be a team effort in order to be effective.

WHAT MISTAKES LEAD YOU TO YOUR SUCCESS?

Having been trained in Western Medicine and raised in its culture, I never explored other avenues of correcting health issues. I was drawn to only participate in Western Medicine and have extensive training in emergency and trauma training. When I became ill, I did not think to explore what was out of balance other than my physical body. I thought I was managing my stress appropriately and effectively by working out and interacting with friends and doing fun things. I only thought of exploring other avenues after going to all the specialists recommended for my specific symptoms, and not finding any answers while my health continued to decline until I became bedridden and unable to effectively communicate on my own. What I discovered was another whole world of options and began studying, in depth, Natural Medicine and specifically Chinese Medicine and how important it is to look at the body from a holistic perspective, looking at the emotional, mental, and spiritual aspects as well as the physical. What I discovered was that my physical body collapsed due to an extensive imbalance in the emotional component of my whole body and how the mental component of my whole body blocked me from recognizing it in the early stages where I could have managed it and my whole body would not have totally collapsed. However, due to my personal experience and my desire to understand why my body collapsed when I always had exceptional health, I have been able to help hundreds of people gain their health back when there was no one in their arena who had answers for their failing health, performing more than 15,000 screenings to date, along with consultations and coaching session.

30 Day Challenge

Starting with Day 1, relax, take a few deep breaths to just quiet your mind. Take 1 minute and tap into your body. What are you noticing? Where are you feeling out of balance? Is there a physical imbalance? Is there an emotion that is out of balance? Are you over-thinking something? Is there something in the Spiritual arena that needs your attention? Which area is speaking louder currently? Whichever one is speaking the loudest is the aspect to focus on for the rest of the week. Each day focus on that aspect, adding 1 minute each day for 1 week. So, by Day 7, you will be focusing on that area and symptoms you are noting for 7 minutes. What is within your control to improve or eliminate those symptoms. What are you noticing with your changes?

Week two – do the initial relax and take a few deep breaths to quiet your mind. Then focus on your body to see what it is telling you. What symptom is coming to the forefront? What aspect is it related to? Is it out of balance due to an emotional imbalance, mental imbalance, physical imbalance, or a Spiritual imbalance? Then take 8 minutes to ask what you need to do to improve the imbalance. Again, each day do the same process, adding a minute each day. Note what is improving as well as what hasn't. Ask has anything gotten worse? What can you do now? What is your one next step?

Example: Week One - First day, you notice you are tight in your neck. From 0-10 what is the level of discomfort? Ask yourself, your Guides, God, what is causing this? Is it just a physical issue? Is there an emotional component that needs attention? Is there a mental component? Is there a Spiritual component? Choose to focus on the area that is most prevalent or stands out to be the most important. Let's say you notice there are things you just do not want to look at currently. So, your emotions are out of balance. Second Day, focus on these issues for 2 minutes. Day 3, focus on issue for 3 minutes. And so on. Continue adding 1 minute each day for each day throughout the week.

In Week two, start with relaxing, deep breathing and focusing for a total of 8 minutes. Using the same process you did on Day 1, tap in to see what aspect of your body is out of balance. Ask the same questions. Each day add another minute of time just to relax and pay attention to what is going on with your body, ending with 14 minutes for Day 14. In Week 3, repeat the same process of tapping in. Start with 15 minutes, again adding 1 minute each day for the rest of the month. On the last day of the 30-day Challenge you will be tapping into your body, identifying symptoms you are aware of and asking "What is my one next step, focusing on the aspect of what is out of balance or just needs additional support.

Take the full 30 minutes on Day 30 and really look at where your health was on Day 1 and where you are now. You should notice you are able to identify imbalances quicker, listening to your body is easier and feeling better each day and enjoying the time you have allowed yourself to relax and create more balance in your life.

If, at any time during your 30 days, you have some time left over from listening to your body and clearing the imbalances, take that time to just breathe, meditate, say positive affirmations, and express gratitude. It is scientifically proven you shift at the cellular level when you express gratitude. Enjoy!!

About the Author

Dr. Linda Potts was born in Washington D.C. Grew up in Bowie, Maryland, except for ages 11-14, where she lived in Thailand. She visited several other countries while living there, all of which enriched her life. She was also fortunate to have traveled across the United States many times during her childhood, camping and visiting friends and relatives a long the way. She went to a Boarding Academy for high school and attended Columbia Union College where she got her BS degree in Nursing. Most her clinical experience as a Registered Nurse, was as an Emergency Room/Trauma nurse and held multiple management positions. She received her MBA from Mt. St. Mary's University in Emmitsburg, Maryland. She has received multiple Certifications in the field of Natural Health since starting her own successful business in 2004, along with a Master's in Bioenergetics. She received a Doctorate in Clinical Religious Counseling and Doctorate in Naturopathy and is a Board-Certified Doctor of Natural Medicine.

Besides her business, which she loves, she enjoys gardening, hiking, biking, kayaking, and spending time with her husband and other family members. Life is good is SO many ways!

Contact information

Dr. Linda Potts, DNM, DCRC, MBA, RN
Company: Healing Waters Wellness Center
Email: healingwaters@myactv.net
LinkedIn: www.linkedin.com/in/dr-linda-potts-4a947911
Facebook: www.facebook.com/HealingWatersWellnessCenter

Dedication

---

*This book is dedicated to my son, Quinn, for being the bright light in my world.
To the powerful women behind Powerful Women Today: Carolina Billings and my
sister chapter leaders around the world. You model how compassion and a relentless
pursuit of success (as we have each defined it for ourselves) leads to financial and
emotional independence for ourselves and others.*

We truly are #StrongerTogether.

Marianne Bjelke

INCREASE CONNECTION
WITH EFFECTIVE COMMUNICATION

You may have taken one look at my last name and asked yourself "Be-WHAT?" Well, my friend, you are not alone. But when you ask me "Be-WHAT?" my response will be: "Be happy, be successful, and today let's be better communicators."

Still, for as long as I can remember that last name has stopped people in their tracks. At this point, I have made a game of spotting the shift in facial expression. Whether it is the hotel check-in attendant, an audience member when I am presenting, or the customer service representative at my dealership, the reaction is always the same. The gaze starts as cordial as they turn to read my name from the screen, and then freezes solid as they try to process the unpronounceable.

"B- oh. Um."

"Ba-jelck? No."

"Bah-geckle?"

I used to dread the thought of causing that moment of discomfort in people, where all body movement stops and is replaced by an uncomfortable pause.

But now?

Now, I absolutely love it. Why? Because there is a secret lesson to be learned in moments like this: Every moment of disconnect with another can become an opportunity to forge a bond. Whether the disconnect is the result of a debate of fiercely opposite philosophies, or as common as using a slang term known only to a part of your audience. Displaying understanding, even in moments of disagreement, and a willingness to listen, even if you are not in agreement, sets the stage for authentic communication to begin.

In every potential hiccup in communication there is an opportunity to create a deeper connection with that person. For example, at that moment when I see the furrowed brow of someone seeing my impossible name for the first time, I get the opportunity to be a problem solver. "It's pronounced bee-ell-kuh. It's Norwegian." And suddenly, everything is ok! You are guided past this unexpected bump in your routine, simply by answering the question you have not yet been asked. What might have resulted in a screeching halt to our communication has instead become a common ground for us to connect.

As an entrepreneur, you have a built-in way to form deep and meaningful connections with your ideal prospects and audiences: your message. Simply speaking, your message is your unique value proposition: "What do you do, who do you do it for, and what problem does it solve." This foundation of your message is often reflected in your Mission and Vision statements and in the Avatar Profile of your ideal customer.

From there, we build the effective phrasing and framing of your message, tailored to your target audience, to exponentially increase the impact you have on your clients, your prospects, and your tribe. Remember, your audience composition may change with each speaking event, each training or workshop, and each sales presentation you give.

Finding clarity in your message starts with clearly defining your mission and vision as an entrepreneur. For increased impact and success, and to position yourself for growth, all of your communications should be in alignment with your mission and vision.

To create your Mission Statement, simply answer these questions:
- WHAT do you do? WHAT problem do you solve?
- HOW do you do it? HOW are you different? HOW are you better?
- WHO do you do it for? WHO is your ideal customer?
- To create your Vision Statement, define WHERE do see your effort ideally taking you in five, ten, fifty years. In other words:

▢ WHAT do you want to accomplish?

▢ By WHEN?

Your message, when carefully crafted, will:

▢ Reflect your Mission and Vision.

▢ Use language that speaks directly to the goals, values, priorities, and motivations of your audience.

▢ Make your listener feel that they have something in common with you.

▢ Authentically present your experience, personality, and unique skillset

▢ Encourage continued engagement.

Here are a few factors to consider when you want to increase the impact of your message:

Word Choice: Something as small as one single word holds the potential to shut down communication before it even has a chance to begin. If you are using a term that may be foreign to even a small part of your listening audience, take the time to define the meaning and context the first time you introduce the term. For example, you may expect a group from a specific industry to understand the slang terms of that industry. The term "grip" has a different meaning to a group from the film industry than it might have to a group of athletes. Chances are that your audience may be comprised of individuals from a cross-section of demographics, interests, and experiences. Clarifying the meaning of the term in those situations where it is possible to interpret the term a different way will help you build connection and understanding with your listeners.

Body movement and positioning: Adjusting your body language can strengthen your communication and help you make a better impression in all kinds of social and professional settings. Facial expressions, hand gestures, and posture all communicate certain meanings. When your body language agrees with your words, what you say is much more powerful. Hold an open posture with head up and shoulders back.

Keep gestures limited to accentuating points of your story and be sure your viewers can clearly see them. If presenting virtually, keep your hands from getting too close to the camera – it can have the same effect as getting too close to someone or invading their personal space. Your gestures should have meaning and only be used to intentionally accent specific points of your presentation.

Avoid nervous gestures. When not using intentional gestures, keep your arms at your sides. For many speakers, this takes practice before it becomes comfortable. If it helps, pretend you are holding onto 5-pound weights. This simple imagery tricks your body into keeping your arms and hands still.

Also, ask yourself "What is my listener's body language telling me?" Are your listeners engaged with you or are they multitasking? If the latter, employ techniques to encourage participation. Survey the audience with a poll or a show of hands. Mention an individual as an example – when they hear their name they will perk up and pay attention. Add comedy – nothing garners attention and connection quite like shared laughter.

Eye Contact: In the live setting, eye contact while presenting is accomplished by looking around the room, reading the expressions of your audience. In the virtual setting, eye contact with your remote participants is achieved by ensuring you are looking at the camera. When you as a speaker are looking at an image of participants on your screen, the participants observe you looking away. By looking into the camera, your audience feels that you are making eye contact and presenting directly to them, individually.

But how might we observe the reactions and expressions of our virtual audience? Professional speakers employ a variety of tricks like using a second monitor, positioned behind the camera, with the attendees shown on gallery view. When recording shows where there is no live audience, putting attention-getting sticky notes or pictures around the camera lens can ensure you maintain that eye contact. There are even special tools that allow you to position your external camera in the middle of your screen instead of resting at the top. Use whichever trick makes the most sense for your presentation style and environment.

Content: Start strong. The first few minutes are critical for capturing your audience's attention. This is the critical time where your audience gets to know you, like you, and trust you. You can lead with an interesting statistic relevant to the problem that you solve for your audience, or a question that will stir up their curiosity.

Tell stories. You can liven up any subject by throwing in some characters and a plot. Draw from your own personal experience or find relevant material in current events and pop culture.

Having trouble creating content for your presentation? Try the 30-Days to a Kick-Ass Presentation challenge in this book!

Pop culture or historical references: Nothing unites us like a shared experience or story. Historical events, movies and shows, and music offer an opportunity to quickly establish rapport with strangers. Before introducing such a reference to support your message, ask: Does my audience have the same familiarity with the subject as I do, or do I need to give some back story to make sure everyone is on a level playing field? Further, can I be sure they feel the same way about this reference as I do, or might I be potentially creating an unintentional division or disagreement with my point?

Similar to using slang, certain references can alienate a part of your audience who may not be "in the know." Does that mean these should be avoided altogether? Not necessarily. Let's say you want to share a story about a television show from a by-gone era. You can always add a few phrases that summarize the show and the context. Just add a few sentences starting with: "For those of you who may not be familiar with _____, it was set in (time/place), and everyone in those days would (common reaction to plot/character)." This not only gets your audience familiar with the context of what you are about to share, but it also strengthens your bond because you have already shared about a topic that has had an influence on you.

Communication styles (projective): Direct communicators like to get to the point quickly but can sometimes be perceived as being rude. Initiating communicators like to socialize first and share stories first but may be seen as attention-seeking. Supportive communicators are often calm and steady but may be viewed as indecisive. Analytical communicators are often precise and data-driven, but that can lead to being considered unrelatable. Every style has its strength and its weakness. Are you maximizing the traits of your preferred communication style to add impact to your message?

Bonus: What is your communication style? Take the assessment here: www.BeWhatNow.com/My-Communication-Style

Listening styles (receptive): The style we prefer to communicate and the style we prefer to listen to is often the same, but for some people, differences can occur. When crafting your message, do you consider the preferred listening style of your audience when crafting your message? How would phrasing your message differ if you presented it to a group of elementary teachers (typically "supportive") as compared to an audience of computer programmers (typically "analytical")?

Learning styles (integrating): Use a variety of media and senses to learn the information. Reading information can be effective, but it is more effective if you read it to yourself or hear it read aloud? Does your audience prefer to listen to a podcast or watch a video?

How do you handle addressing an audience with a blend of learning styles? Consider the learning style of your listener when crafting your message. Pick terms that resonate with each of those styles and use them all in your written and presented work. Fun fact: the previous sentence intentionally included terms that would appeal to the kinesthetic learner ("pick"), the audio learner ("resonate"), and the visual learner ("written").

Active Listening: Everyone wants to be heard, and effective communication is a two-way street. Others will notice that you are listening to them and will go away from your conversations thinking what a great communicator you are when all you did was listen. Your listening skills are even more important than your speaking skills. After all, how will you know what you should say, how you should say it, and when, if you haven't effectively listened and observed?

In the virtual or live setting, whether you are speaking to an audience of one, ten, hundreds or more, the same principles hold true. The potential to invite a deeper connection and to exponentially increase our impact exists with every encounter. Once we learn to recognize the opportunities, we can then make simple adjustments to how we deliver our message, opening the gates to true and meaningful connections.

Being an effective communicator is not easy, but YOU are up to the challenge. Working with a communication strategist can help you identify both the visible and the hidden opportunities to strengthen your communication and presentation skills. Want to add impact to YOUR message? Apply for a complimentary strategy call with me: www.BusinessCommunicationStrategy.com

We'll talk soon!

30 Day Challenge

THIRTY-DAYS TO KICK-ASS PRESENTATION CHALLENGE

This simple-to-do challenge will pay off handsomely if you are consistent, persistent, and open to accept yourself as you are with the goal of improving your presentation skills. Every day you will:

1. Record yourself speaking.
2. Listen to / Watch your recording.
3. Identify small improvements you will make for the next day.

Sit in front of your Zoom camera or record yourself speaking into your phone – whatever is easiest for you. Start out small – even just a few minutes. You can pretend you are addressing a client, a club, or a conference.

When we start to work together for the first time, many of my presentation coaching clients tell me "Marianne, I hate the way I sound" or "I do not like watching myself." And it is true, we can be our own worst critics. The only way to get over the hurdle of being uncomfortable when listening to, or watching yourself, is to listen to and watch yourself more. Every time you listen to and watch yourself, you will learn more accurately how your audience sees you and how you can make small changes to improve your performance.

Every 5 days add in the next ingredient to crafting your Kick-Ass Presentation. You got this!

DAY 1

Introduce yourself. The hardest thing to do is to get in front of the audience and start speaking. Make it easier by speaking on the topic you know best – yourself! Share who you are, what you do, and the problem that you solve for others.

DAY 5

Share your knowledge. After your introduction comes the part where you share your knowledge. What do you want to teach your audience? Pick 3 points. (No more, no less)

DAY 10

Pacing, Vocal Variety. Listen to what you have so far. Practice slowing down when sharing the summary of each key point. Practice repeating statements that you want to be sure your audience receives. Practice raising and lowering your voice at certain times as if you are sharing a secret or making an exciting announcement. Your material may be familiar to you, but it will be new to your audience. Variations in volume and speed help your audience retain the information better.

DAY 15

Determine your Call-To-Action. How do you want your audience to engage with you after your talk? Do you want them to visit your website? Sign up for your newsletter? Buy your book or course? This part goes after your knowledge-share and before your closing statements.

DAY 20

Strengthen your closing and opening statements. A strong open gets the audience's attention right away. Ask a question or share a relevant statistic. A strong close will stay with the audience long after your presentation is over. Challenge them to commit to a course of action or ask them to imagine what their life would look like upon successfully deploying the key points you have just shared.

DAY 25

Appeal to the variety of listeners in your audience. We experience the world through our senses. Go through your content so far and determine where you might add or substitute words that are more sensory and evocative. Anyone can share that they were "in the park." There is much greater effect on your audience when you describe the smell of the grass/flowers, the sound of the nearby birds/traffic/stream, the heat or cold of the wind/sun/rain. This also serves the purpose of appealing to the different learning styles that people in your audience prefer. Allowing your listener to take in your words more visually, more audibly, more kinesthetically, results in increased connection.

DAY 30

Take it on the road. Find a colleague or a coach who will listen to your presentation (deliver it live) and give you feedback. Not everyone is comfortable giving feedback so be sure to ask them specifically: What did you like? What could I improve? What parts made an impact and why?

About the Author

Marianne Bjelke (bee-ell-kuh), *The Business Communication Strategist*, is the host and mentor to the very first Powerful Women Today chapter in the United States, located in the beautiful high-desert region of Albuquerque, New Mexico.

The founder of Strategic Business Solutions Consulting, Marianne understands how the nuances of communication impact running a profitable business. Her clients turn to her for increased awareness of perspective bias, communication styles, generational influences, and more – awareness which helps them blast through the often unseen barriers to true communication and impact.

A stand-up comedian in NYC at age 21, she settled down and opened her first successful business, Herb'N Trends – a retail herb, tea, and gift shop, at just 25 years old. Moving cross-country two years later allowed Marianne to pursue a new passion; programming and software development. She quickly grew this into an executive management career, enjoying over 15 years in healthcare information management before striking out on her own. Marianne has successfully managed award-winning 7-figure revenue-generating projects from concept and design, through the development stages and into launch.

Working with cross-functional teams ignited her passion for helping ALL project stakeholders (developers, designers, marketing teams, end users, and executive stakeholders) speak the same mission-driven language to effectively define goals and complete projects on time, on spec, and on budget.

She and her son live with their dogs in the foothills of the beautiful Sandia Mountain in Albuquerque, New Mexico. In her spare time, she enjoys laughter, whisky tasting, and soaking in natural hot springs.

Contact Information

Marianne Bjelke

Company: Strategic Business Solutions Consulting

Email: marianne@powerfulwomentoday.com

LinkedIn: www.linkedin.com/in/mariannebjelke

Facebook: www.facebook.com/bewhatnow

Website: www.bewhatnow.com

Dedication

I dedicate this chapter to all women who are out there doing there best,

get knocked down, and continue to choose to move forward.

Mindy Gillis

LEADING SELF

Hello and welcome. In this month we will focus on how you lead yourself and how you show up to the world. I have spent my entire career working on my own leadership and cultivating how I want to show up to others and how I lead myself. So many of us have allowed life to just happen to us and we wonder why we haven't reached our goals and dreams. We must be intentional about how we show up to the world and how we want people to perceive us. Perception is reality and we have to learn how other people perceive us. Do they see us as a thought leader? A leader of self? A leader in your industry? This is where we must take a few steps back and really take a good look at ourselves and ask for feedback, reflect on how we've shown up, and really get to know who we really are. This can seem like a scary task, but it is a gift that you can give yourself that will help to propel you forward towards your goals. If you don't know what your blind spots are then how can you fix them? Everything that I will ask you to do are things that I have gone through myself. I have overcome many obstacles in my life, and I have learned and grown throughout my career. I have a passion to help others identify how they show up and how they can lead themselves.

Four Pillars of Leading Self
YOUR WEEKLY ACTIVITIES TO LEVELING UP YOUR LEADERSHIP

WEEK 1 – SELF-AWARENESS

Self-awareness takes a journey. There is no endpoint because we are constantly changing. It is important to consistently ask for feedback from those who you trust and will provide you with honest and transparent feedback. Feedback is a gift. When someone gives you feedback it is very hard for them to provide real honest feedback. Therefore, when you ask for feedback, it is imperative that you don't try to excuse your behavior or provide reasons why you are the way you are. That is like throwing away a gift that someone has given you. The best way to respond to feedback is to simply say "Thanks for the feedback". This way of responding to feedback creates an open line of communication between you and the person providing you feedback. Feedback is a gift. Highly successful people ask for feedback and ask for it often.

Week 1 Activity

- Ask those who know you well, at least five people, the following questions:
- What do I do well?
- What might I be doing that is getting in my way of being successful?
- What is your wish for me?

WEEK 2 – DISCOVERING YOUR VISION

Discovering who you want to be is the first step to how you show up in the world. We must also set a vision for our life before we can show up every day to make our vision happen. If you don't have a vision then how will we know what to focus on? Often we end up spending time on things that don't take us towards our goals and it wastes time, energy, and money. A life and business vision helps you to get clear on what you want so that you know where to focus your energy, time, and money to propel you on your journey of emotional and financial freedom.

Week 2 Activity

Imagine that you can see into the future and five years from now a famous writer is writing about you and your accomplishments. This is a huge win for you and you are extremely excited for this article because it will propel your business and set you up for financial and emotional freedom. What would you say to the following questions? Keep in mind to think BIG!

- Tell me your story and how you got to this amazing place with your career/business?
- Who helped you achieve your goals along the way?
- What did you do when things got tough and you wanted to walk away?
- What do you want the world to know about you and how you've made an impact? What kind of impact did you make?
- What do you believe in?

WEEK 3: CREATING MEASURABLE GOALS

Now that you've seen into your future and you can see what you want to be, this is where you can start breaking things down into smaller steps and create a plan on how you can make your vision come to life. We'll be working on creating short term goals and creating a vision board. When you put your goals down on paper and you make it where you see it everyday, it will help you with your own accountability.

Week 3 Activity

Day One: To get to your five year vision, what would you want to have accomplished in three years?

- ☐ Where will you be?
- ☐ What will you be doing?
- ☐ What will your business look like?

Day Two: To get to your five year vision, what would you want to have accomplished in one year?

- ☐ Where will you be?
- ☐ What will you be doing?
- ☐ What will your business look like?

Day Three: To get to your five year vision, what would you want to have accomplished in six months?

- ☐ Where will you be?
- ☐ What will you be doing?
- ☐ What will your business look like?

Day Four: To get to your five year vision, what can you do tomorrow to get started towards your goals?

- ☐ What obstacles might get in your way?
- ☐ What keeps you from taking the next best step?
- ☐ How might you create an accountability group to help you get to your goals?

Day Five: Reflect back on the past three weeks and write down your thoughts regarding the process.

WEEK 4 – OVERCOMING SELF-DEFEATING THOUGHTS

This might be one of the toughest weeks for you. This is where you go back over your activities and write down the self-defeating thoughts that came up for you while you were working through the activities. Often, it is the negative thoughts that ruminate in our minds that keep us from reaching our vision and goals. These thoughts might come from what you were told when you were growing up or they are thoughts that we've created as a protection mechanism but now they are self-sabotaging. I urge you to take this activity seriously and reflect on what thoughts might be holding you back. Once you are able to recognize these thoughts then you can choose to reframe the thoughts and create a new montra for your life.

Week 4 – Activity

Reflect back on this month's activities. Write down any self-defeating thought that you had. Then write down the reframed thought.

Example:

- Activity
- Self-Defeating Thought
- Reframed Thought

WEEK ONE: SELF-AWARENESS

I don't want to ask my friends these questions. I am afraid of what they might say. I know this is out of my comfort zone. I chose to believe that feedback is a gift and this will help me grow so that I can find financial and emotional freedom.

WEEK TWO: CREATING YOUR VISION

This is too hard. How can I possibly do this. I don't even know what tomorrow looks like. I chose to think bigger than I ever thought that I could. I chose to not allow self-defeating thoughts get in my way. I have a lot to offer.

WEEK THREE: CREATING MEASURABLE GOALS

I don't like writing down my goals. They are so hard to come up with, especially thinking five years out. I don't know if I am good enough. Without a plan, how can I reach my vision and goals. What do I have to lose? I am strong and capable of reaching my vision.

Thank you for taking this journey with me. You've done a lot of hard work. You've just received over $3,000 worth of coaching from me. Go back through these exercises once every six months to refresh your ideas as you continue to refine and get clear on your vision.

If you'd like to go deeper with this work and could use some help, please feel free to reach out to me for a free 30 minute discovery call. Email me at mindy@mindycoaching.com and feel free to review my LinkedIn references www.linkedin.com/in/mindygillis

I look forward to hearing how these activities helped you and coaching you through this process. Email me today at mindy@mindycoaching.com Wishing you amazing success on your journey.

About the Author

Mindy's Executive Coaching, LLC is about developing a creative partnership with clients capitalizing on their potential igniting creativity, leadership, passion, and drive. My passion is around executive coaching and leadership consulting with leaders and their leadership teams to improve their leadership capabilities to achieve professional, team, organizational, and personal goals. My niche is developing diverse physician leaders. Assisting clients to harness their greatness and discovering unrealized talents.

Helping people harness their greatness through various coaching topics:
  [] Leadership effectiveness
  [] Emotional Intelligence
  [] Interpersonal intelligence/skills

- Crucial Conversations - including holding difficult conversations

- Resiliency/Burnout

- Transitions in leadership roles

- Time and prioritization management

- Career development

- Agile/Adaptability quotient

- Leadership workshops

- Board retreats

- Team retreats

Mindy Gillis, MEd, PCC

Mindy's Executive Coaching, LLC

Certified Professional Coach with ICF, PCC

Certified Executive Coach, CEC

Certified Empowerment Coach with Powerful Women Today

Ceritified Visionary Leadesrhip Coach, CVLC

Certified MentorCoach, CMC

Contact Information
Mindy Gillis, MEd, PCC
Company: Mindy's Executive Coaching
Email: mindy@mindycoaching.com
LinkedIn: www.linkedin.com/in/mindygillis
Twitter: www.twitter.com/mindygillis
Website: www.mindygillis.com

Dedication

This book is dedicated to my boys: Cason, Sawyer and Wylder. Sometimes you drive me to the brink of insanity and then three simple words come out of your mouth and I realize what I do is for the three of you, "I love you". Make all your dreams happen because you each have the courage, will and determination that you get from your mommy.

Amber Trail

*I am and will always be forever grateful for my life journey
and passion for human resources.*

Women need to lead the world with their actions and their voice. Women have broken barriers over the last century but it's still not enough. We have made an impact, but we have not changed the world yet. We still struggle with the mindset that women are not equals. We suffer through unequal pay, glass ceilings and the fact that most individuals think we must pick between being mothers and having a career. I'm here to tell you that we don't have to be one or the other. We can do both!

I am a mom of three boys and very much career minded. I have never once neglected my children or their needs. Women need to stop thinking that they must choose between their happiness and their children's happiness. It's simply not true. We have the power to succeed in the workforce, provide for our families, and still play an active role in our children's lives.

Often, I've heard in the workplace, "we've been so flexible with you because you have kids". What kind of statement is that to make? This was said to me when I was working evenings and weekends to make up for any time, I had to leave to take care of a sick kid or drop them off at daycare or school late because of a snowstorm. I was averaging five hours more a week than any other individual without kids. Please tell me how flexible you are with me now?

The problem comes in the fact that most women let these comments be made without standing up for themselves. For a long time, I let the comments be made because I was too afraid of the repercussions if I did in fact stand up for myself. What would happen? Would I lose my job? There comes a time when you finally get fed up and let it out. Let it all out. When you finally do, it feels fantastic! When you get to the point when you don't care about the repercussions, you've finally found your voice because you know deep in your heart that you are standing up for what is right. Blessings come after that moment. Things start to come into your life that you never imagined possible.

Sometimes the closest people to us are the most critical of all our actions. I know firsthand that this can be so difficult to overcome, and to think that you can do so much more than what they say you can or can't do. Stop believing the crap. It may be a spouse, a parent, a sibling, or a best friend who is filling your head with negative nonsense.

Write down a list of all the things you want to be. All of them. Instead of saying "I want to be" say "I am". Read this list every morning to yourself in front of the mirror. It may seem ridiculous at first but don't stop saying those things to yourself until you truly believe them. If you're thinking about them, they are true. You just need to know that you're worth it and you have a voice. Break the barriers and prove the naysayers wrong.

Whether a woman wants to start a side business for some extra cash, a full-time entrepreneurship or excel higher than ever in the workforce – they need to stop listening to the background noise of "you're a mom, you can't do both". Yes, you can. Moms are the world's best multi-taskers. Find your support system, because you will need one, and go for it. There are no glass ceilings in this world. Think it, plan it, and do it.

WHAT MISTAKES LEAD YOU TO YOUR SUCCESS?

Divorce. I removed myself from a completely dependent marriage that was absolutely toxic. I grew up thinking I always needed a man to support me. I grew up with the mindset that a man would make my dreams come true. Not that you could do it yourself but that I had to have a man do it all for me. So. Not. True. Seriously, why do we teach our children this terrible demeaning mindset?

When my mom passed away in 2017, I was newly married, pregnant and out of a job. I felt the world collapse around me. A week before my youngest son was born, I started job searching. Determined to find something to make my own money again. Three days after I had my son, I was sitting in a conference room for a panel interview for an HR Director role. I nailed it. The moment I stepped into that role; I knew I was meant for so much more that life had to offer.

After the company started downsizing due to layoffs and reduction in manufacturing products, I decided I needed to be more involved in HR. I went to the owner and discussed my options. He spoke highly about consulting. I thought, why not! The HR Trail, LLC was born in May of 2019. I had no idea what I was doing. No one in my family ever owned a business and everyone I knew thought I was crazy. I realized I was not surrounding myself around the right kind of people if I wanted to be successful.

I started searching for groups. I found a women's group that I joined and met several life-long friends. These women are the best friends I have ever had. This then pushed me to start tackling more obstacles because owning a business is no walk in the park. It's hard! I started researching other women's groups because I wanted to be surrounded by women who owned who they were and thrived off success. I found Powerful Women Today. Here I am now. I am always striving harder and harder to be the best human I can possibly be. To show everyone around me, in this small little town I live in, that women can be powerful and successful and still have an amazing love life! We no longer have to choose between being a good mom or being a career woman. We can be both. As a mom of three boys, I can tell you that my boys see the best in me because I am doing what I love.

30 Day Challenge

Thirty-Days to Rocking
A MOM/WORK LIFE

This simple challenge entails easy to put into place steps that allow you to not have "mom guilt" over being a high performing individual while still rocking it in the workplace. Every day you will want to find time to focus on you, create new habits and most importantly, give yourself some grace!

Follow this simple step by step guide to truly make a difference in your own life. I, myself, am a very high performing individual. I am also my own worst enemy. I struggle keeping up with being an active mom, business owner and spending time for myself. We live in a world where many negative thoughts surround us by what others from the outside of our lives may say or see. What they don't know is that you are doing the best you can. But what if you could do better? There's always room for improvement. Start here.

Day 1

Today I want you to look yourself in the mirror every single morning, I want you to really look deep into your eyes and tell yourself that you love the person in the mirror and that you are a rockstar.

Day 2-5

Every morning, I want you to start a list of what you want in your life. Create your very own vision board. Create statements that are serving you as if they already happened. For example, "I am an International Best-Selling Author" – by the way, I wrote this down and guess what…. three months later, it happened! Make a list that is exactly what you want in your life.

Day 6-10

Self-care. Write down one thing you can do every single day to show yourself that you love yourself. This could be as simple as taking 10 minutes to read something that interests you. It can also be a very expensive massage. I know we can't realistically do this every day but maybe once a month, right? Use this list when you run out of ideas later on. Every single day, you need to do something to take care of yourself.

Day 11-15

Time management. Are you shutting off work at a certain time of the day? If not, these next few days I want you to set a timer for yourself and set the notifications for your phone on silent. Turn them off! I had a bad habit of answering emails all hours of the day and that set a standard that was turning me into someone I did not want to be. Your time is important. Especially when you have children. Spend quality time with your kids, as much as you can.

Day 16-20

Learn when to say no. I used to say "yes" to everything. I mean everything. It made me resent the people I was saying yes to. It wasn't their fault, it was mine. I had to make some really hard decisions to cut people and tasks out of my life. They were not serving me. You will make some people angry but that's okay because they are not you. They are not living your life. So, what is not serving you?

Day 21-25

Professional and personal development. I try to spend 20 minutes every day on developing me. Whether that is reading a book, listening to a podcast or tuning into a webinar. Find something that you can dive into every day for only 20 minutes, 30 minutes max, that will serve you.

Day 26-30

Repeat. I want you to repeat these steps every single day. Start small and simple. Continue to add on to your daily routine slowly. Start with a simple, "I love you" in the mirror. Glance at your vision board every day, do something that takes care of you, manage your time effectively, say no and spend a little bit every day on personal and professional development.

You are a powerhouse. Do not let anyone tear down your dreams!

About the Author

Amber Trail, MBA, SHRM-CP is the founder of The HR Trail, LLC. The HR Trail transformed from a consulting firm to a mentoring firm for other HR professionals worldwide. Amber is also an international best-selling author, international speaker, certified life coach, certified women empowerment coach, certified goal success coach and the face behind the "HR without Borders" podcast. With over 13 years of progressive corporate HR experience and a master's degree in Business Administration, Amber brings her passion and knowledge of human resources to many other determined HR professionals worldwide. She lives in a very rural area of Pennsylvania, USA with her family.

Contact Information

Amber Trail, MBA, SHRM-C
Company: The HR Trail, LLC
Email: amber@thehrtrail.com
LinkedIn: www.linkedin.com/in/ambertrail
Facebook: www.facebook.com/thehrtrail
Website: www.thehrtrail.com

Dedication

_____

To all the warrior women...love on

Piper Dominguez

Have you ever woken up one day not recognizing who you are anymore? Have you ever caught yourself dreaming of a future that seems like an impossible reality? Do you have big dreams but feel guilty about imagining those same big dreams?

From the outside, maybe your life looks pretty good. As I look at my own life and how blessed I am to have a supportive and loving family, beautiful children, I get to live in an amazingly beautiful place and do the things that nourish me, my life has not always felt like this.

I spent many years feeling an underlying sense of guilt for daring to desire more while from the outside my life seemed pretty amazing. I had an innate sense I was here for more than what I was living yet felt guilty for wanting more. I kept thinking I should be happy and grateful for what I have. I often thought, who was I to ask for more; who was I to take time for myself in order to really go for what I want; I should just be happy with what I have. However, there was something missing and I couldn't quite place my finger on what it was. All I knew was that it felt like a hollow part of myself. The result of living my life in this way was getting up each day to a life that was busy but didn't feel full or nourishing, it was mundane and it was draining me. The longer I ignored the call for more, the louder it got. I began to resent those closest to me and I felt like I was falling apart inside. It took having to go through a major upheaval in my life to snap me back to reality and decide that I was no longer willing to tolerate my life as it was, I needed to make some adjustments.

I realized that life is just a moment in time, but I did not want to have that moment pass knowing I had another choice and didn't take it. I did not want to come to the end of my existence with regret. Instead I wanted to live my life fully expressed and to life's fullest potential. I once heard a teaching story where someone was given a divine purpose and while they lived their life doing all kinds of amazing things, they did not do the one thing they had been sent to do. The ripple effects of that was like they hadn't lived at all. When I heard this, I realized I could no longer ignore the calling to step into the life I had come here to live and be the person I was being asked to become. I had to make a choice and take different actions despite all the fear that was coming up around it.

It all started to become more conscious when I woke up feeling like I had lost my mojo somewhere along the way of motherhood. I had become that mother I thought I would never be. I sat feeling disenchanted with our choices for the day...do we go to the zoo again or to the playground or to the museum for the umpteenth time? Where had my passion and zest for life gone? I wasn't sure but it was obviously not present and neither was I. Shortly prior my life had been turned upside down when my mother passed at 64 years of age. She was my rock, my best friend, and even though I had expected this it did not make it any easier when she was gone.

This was the wakeup call I needed to realize how far from my center I had drifted.

I realized just how far from my dreams and goals I had come. My compass had turned 180 degrees in the opposite direction from where I started and at the same time, I wasn't sure how long I had been walking unconsciously through life. I became aware that life was leading me instead of being the captain of my own ship. I found myself looking at this person looking back at me in the mirror not sure which one of us was doing the looking. I had become a drifter traveling without a destination searching for home but without land in sight.

It made me question this longing inside of me that drives this search for something more. It made me question my choices, my paths, my experiences. It made me question my story. Slowly the answers to all these unanswered questions I was holding were starting to stir within and come into knowing.

I believe the universe is constantly reflecting back to us that which we need to address, and at the same time revealing clues to our questions. This series of thoughts and questioning is not new for me. It seems to constantly be at the forefront of my thought process. However, when it becomes more than just a thought process, I know it is a call to re-center and refocus on my dreams and my goals. It is an opportunity to change my story.

Sometimes I still catch myself going through the motions of life and I find myself getting caught up in the mundane day to day-ness of it all and I forget about why I am here. This journey has been about putting myself back into the equation of my life so that I can consciously step into my life purpose. I want to reawaken to the possibilities of my existence, to feel alive, to be reminded once again that it all starts with me. It is about resetting my inner compass and getting quiet so that I can listen to my heart's desire. As Carl Jung said, "Your visions will become clear only when you look into your own heart. Who looks outside, dreams; who looks inside, awakens."

So how do you change your story when you have come so far from what you thought was your story? How do you change directions when you don't know where you want to go? How do you know where your true north is when it feels like your compass is broken? How do you know what you want it to feel like if you don't know how you feel?

It happens in the same way that a caterpillar doesn't think about its own transformation, but fully trusts even in the darkness through its metamorphosis. The challenge for humans is you often get labelled and put into boxes. For some time, my label had been "just a mom". That is how I recognized myself and how others painted me. Even though innately I knew being a mom was just a small part of a bigger picture, an integral part of a bigger purpose, it wasn't complete. However, when the world sees you as one thing it can be challenging to re-educate others on roles and identity and create a new story for yourself without first getting lost in the pages.

The thing is, we all have a story. Your history is a collection of pieces that make up who you are and offers a sense of purpose and belonging. It is a mosaic of your life that creates a beautiful story book. However, what happens when your story doesn't feel exciting? Maybe your story feels broken? Maybe yours is missing chapters? How do you put the pieces back together?

I would say that most women have chinks in their mosaic or torn pages in their story and yet these same pieces and pages make up the whole of who you are. Many women would probably like to swap out for kinder, more joyful, more fitting pieces, however the truth is that those chinks are what add depth, they are what allow you to decide to grow or wither, they are the turning points that give you choice and help wake you up. They are unique to you and your book of life.

I had reached a place in my story though that didn't feel true or authentic. I was no longer holding the pen and I realized if my life was going to change then I had to once again become the scribe. Unlike the butterfly, who from the beginning knows its life mission and gracefully evolves to unfurl its wings, I had forgotten my mission and become disconnected from my story. I had been talked out of it, talked myself out of it, journeyed away from it, danced around it, until the spark within, that seed planted before birth, could no longer be contained within the confines of this body, by my own cocoon. There is too much to share, to offer, to bring forth from my being. It is time to stop playing small and step into the magnitude of my soul, to step into greater service having allowed for the discovery of the Way towards my own metamorphosis. It was time to start a new chapter.

Up until now I have allowed the world to tell me who I was and write my story for me. I hadn't spent long enough in my cocoon dissolving the untrue parts of myself so that I could not only claim this path but I could flourish. So much fear stood in my way...fear of failure, fear of seeming like a fraud, fear of not knowing enough, not being enough, and so on. For every reason why I knew I should do this, there were ten more fear-based reasons why I shouldn't. I have put up blocks, barriers, excuses to avoid feeling uncomfortable and stay safe.

However, fear can be one of our greatest teachers and when I am not sure about something it is either because I really should do it or I really shouldn't, but I won't know until I do the thing. I have been called to this path and challenged to do things in a way that I am not familiar with. I am being asked to step way outside my comfort zone and stretch, to stop messing around and claim my worth, my purpose and my truth.

You see, I have learned something in this life... that I CAN have it all. I have learned that I can be a great mom and a successful coach. I can mess up and recover. I can live a deeply spiritual life and still be IN this world. Life is a both/and, not an either/or. I have said yes to something that is so much bigger than me and I am still trying to find my way with it but that is all part of the journey and the evolution. The question is, do I have the courage to step into the unknown without having a clear vision of who I will become on the other end?

Going through an upheaval in life, as I did with my mom, sent me spiraling and I struggled to regain footing and walk towards my true north. In the process of transformation that occurs through grief there is a purification, like being washed many times over by the waves of the ocean. Within that space of being uncomfortable and moving through the heartache, a blossoming took place with me. Like the caterpillar dissolving itself within its cocoon to fully take on a new form, from that blossoming a space opened up. It was as if my mom handed over a baton, not with what was left undone in her life, but with a space of unlimited potential and possibility to fully step into who I am being called to be, to fully break open and spread my wings. I was being called to look at the hollow place within myself and find my light within that space.

For so long I watched my mom struggle with the same internal conflicts that have plagued me around knowing there was much more but not knowing how to navigate towards it. I saw being reflected in me the same self-doubt, the judgement, the high expectations, the perfectionism, the great desire to create beauty in this world but at the expense of my own well-being and life mission. As I sat in the void, I realized she was offering me a blessing of love. She was showing me how to get out of my own way and go towards what is important, to go towards love. Love is what I was missing. More importantly, self-love.

Self-love is self-care and vice versa. Self-love is a deep form of self-care. It is a WAY of nurturing and taking care of yourself so that you can show up more fully and authentically on the most fundamental levels in your life. It is about being in ALIGNMENT with who you are and what you are doing in this world. It is about showing up AUTHENTICALLY and FULLY EXPRESSED. You cannot do that if you are not clear on who you are, what you want, how you move within your life. If you are not taking care of yourself in the most basic and fundamental levels of life, then you are not writing your own story but rather you are allowing the circumstances of life to determine your fate.

Part of the challenge a lot of women face is there seems to be this idea that taking care of yourself and self-love is somehow selfish. Katie Reed said, "Self-care is giving the world the best of you, instead of what's left of you." Many women seem to think that putting everyone else before themselves is somehow serving. Yet, how can you serve if you are not filling your own cup. Before deciding to really claim my life for me, I was in a place of filling everyone else's cup. In that space it becomes draining and easy to lose sight of who you really are because you begin to look for love and belonging outside yourself, when it is first and foremost an inside job.

Women have good intentions of taking care of others and it is often from a place of wanting to help and serve, and yet if you are not showing up for yourself and loving yourself first by taking care of your own needs, this can easily turn to resentment, anger, depletion, judgement, exhaustion, and illness. You then start projecting out onto others or drive these feelings deeper within yourself which also isn't healthy. I would like you to challenge the idea that putting yourself first is somehow selfish. It does not mean "mefirst", it means "me too". It means that you are including yourself in the vision you hold for your life.

As you begin to love yourself you also begin to learn what you truly need and what makes you feel most nourished. If we look at the laws of the universe, the law of giving and receiving states that you must give before you can receive so that applies to you as well. You must first give yourself the kind of care you need before you can give it or receive it from someone else with the same love and selflessness that so many women crave.

What might your life look like if you took a little time each day to nurture yourself? How would you show up differently if you first filled your own cup and put your needs at the top of your priority list instead of everyone else's?

If you are struggling with this idea and feel that attending to everyone else's needs is somehow showing up as your best self, I would like to challenge that notion by thinking about it like this. When you are showing in your life and serving from an empty cup, what you are really doing is offering someone the C+ version of yourself instead of the A+ version. Your life will look somewhat similar to what mine did, where I was depleted, unfulfilled, feeling like there was something missing. The other side of that is those who are receiving you from that empty place are also feeling that. It feels so much better when we can give ourselves freely and show up feeling fully nourished.

Part of claiming your true authentic story is also knowing how to find harmony with the pieces that make up your life. How do you balance the inner and the outer without losing yourself in the process? Some would say that there isn't really such a thing as balance and while I agree to a certain extent, I also feel that this is a very black and white way of thinking about things. There is this idea though, that in order to be more successful and have greater well-being and happiness, that some semblance of balance is necessary. A woman who is well balanced and lives a more well balanced life is better able to focus her attention and energy on her goals and take action. However, if you do a google search on finding balance it comes up with about 2,340,000,000 results! That is a lot of people looking for balance in their life! We all know we need it, but it would seem from these results that few people actually experience it in their life or know how to get it.

This is where knowing what you need to re-center and love yourself wholly becomes so essential. It isn't about having perfect balance in your life where all things are equal, but what it is about is knowing what to let go of, what to delegate and what to make more time for. It is about prioritizing your life so that you are living in alignment with your values and if you start to spin out knowing how to get yourself back on track. It is important to explore how you do that uniquely for you and work your inner life to be more in alignment with your outer.

30 Day Challenge

GRATITUDE

I invite you to use this month to anchor into gratitude. Gratitude, when done with sincerity, will change your life. When you are experiencing chaos, discontent, feeling like you lost your mojo, or even when things are seemingly well but there is a desire for more, it is so important to focus on what is present in your life that you can be grateful for. Gratitude opens the doorway to possibility. By offering out thanks, you will begin to attract more of what you are thankful for. Gratitude has a way of lifting your spirit and creating space so that you can view your life from a different perspective.

Consistently practicing gratitude has numerous benefits, including rewiring the brain, shielding you from negativity, enhancing feelings of happiness, reducing stress, and improving your life on so many levels. Neale Donald Walsh said, "The struggle ends when the gratitude begins. You can step out of the struggle by consciously choosing gratitude.

Begin by taking an inventory of your life. This has to be done without shame or judgment, knowing that there is no right or wrong on this journey; what is showing up in your life that is wanting attention? What are the deeper questions seeking answers? What are the stories you have been telling yourself that are no longer serving the vision you are holding for your life? Gratitude takes presence. It requires that you are actively vigilant in seeking that which you want even before it has appeared. "Gratitude is not a passive response to something we have been given, gratitude arises from paying attention, from being awake in the presence of everything that lives within and without us". (David Whyte)

Gratitude is the first step towards opening the heart. What we focus on is what we create. So, if you are worried, anxious or overwhelmed and that is what is consuming the majority of your thoughts, then that is what you will receive more of in your life. You will attract more worry, anxiety and feelings of being overwhelmed. However, what if you could instead experience abundance, grace, joy and feel grateful for all that is? It is not about ignoring the parts of us that are stirred, but it is about deciding how we respond and the meaning you place on whatever might be happening. What if you were to respond with gratitude? How might that change your life?

As William Arthur Ward said, "Gratitude can turn ordinary days into Thanks-givings".

Gratitude is the key to unlocking the field of possibility that is available to everyone. Whenever you are faced with a desire for more but you feel that it is out of reach or not available to you, that is a call to anchor into gratitude. You must feel the sense of gratitude in every part of your being. It isn't enough to just give thanks and continue to hold onto the belief that it isn't part of your reality. Part of the secret of gratitude is emotionalizing it and imagining what you want before you actually see it in your life.

Whatever you desire is available to you here and now. However, you have to practice showing up already in thanks for that which is given. In other words, you must first give your gratitude before being able to fully receive that which you want.

Many of my client sessions start with gratitude and celebration. We begin by focusing our attention on all the big and little things that have occurred during the week and give thanks. It is amazing what opens up for my clients as a result.

I recently experienced some challenges in growing my business. As I worked through where I was resisting and what was showing up for me in the challenge, I realized that I kept getting stuck in the disappointment. I had a big money goal for myself and instead of going to gratitude and anchoring into that, I was allowing myself to stay in the disappointment and lack. I was trying to control the outcome and the how, instead of leaning deeply into faith and gratitude that everything I needed to support my goal was already here and available to me now. Everything is a teaching if you allow it to be but I was not seeing it that way. In my experience, I created a problem when in reality there was no problem at all, just a lack of gratitude. If I had been fully grateful for what the experience was affording me then those small obstacles to my goal would not have stopped me and I would have continued to take action in faith and show up more powerfully. As soon as I shifted into gratitude for my goal, knowing that it was already here, that is when my results started to change.

I share this because it is a simple shift and yet I watch clients and myself occasionally get stuck here and wonder what is happening. When you are in a place of lack it is very difficult to see the opportunities that are right in front of you, in fact you can't see them. When there is a lack of gratitude in your life you will continue to experience and attract more lack, as well as more of what you do not want. The remedy is always gratitude.

As you journey forward, where can you practice greater gratitude? Despite the outcome of your present life and the many other trials, tribulations and struggles you have experienced, can you find something to anchor into where you can express a moment of gratitude? Maybe, it is that you still have a job, or that despite current events there is still hope. Maybe, you have good food on your table or more family time. Maybe, it is a sunset or sunrise that takes your breath away or the quiet stillness of the first snowfall. Whatever it may be, I invite you to take a few moments and relish in one thing that you are genuinely grateful for. Make it a daily habit to seek out the beauty in your life because a glimmer of thanks holds tremendous freedom.

I encourage you to do this as a daily practice in the morning when you get up and as a reflection before going to sleep at night. What are three things daily you can be grateful for? Write them down, keep a journal so that you make it conscious. Feel the thanks in your words of gratitude. Take a moment to breathe it all in and feel it, see it and hear it! As Rumi so beautifully said, "wear gratitude like a cloak and it will feed every corner of your life".

About the Author

Piper Dominguez is an LA-based transformational life coach and personal development expert for women and mompreneurs. She has helped women across the globe create more empowering paradigms for their life by taking control of their mental health. Known as the sage warrior coach, Piper guides women ready to transform their life and business with more ease and grace while overcoming the obstacles that stand in the way of their success. She provides a safe space to help build the emotional strength and confidence to show up authentically and unapologetically in life. Piper believes it is every woman's birthright to live the fullest expression of their life possible.

Piper lives within walking distance to the beach where she enjoys long walks in the sand with her husband and two young boys. She also enjoys traveling, reading, cooking, getting creative and intentionally seeking out the beauty life has to offer.

Contact information

Piper Dominguez

Company: Piper Dominguez Coaching

Email: psdmngz@gmail.com

LinkedIn: www.linkedin.com/in/piper-dominguez-28b89231/

Facebook: www.facebook.com/piper.dominguez

Website: www.piperdominguez.com

Dedication

Dr. Bernell and Betty Jones, Mom and Pop who keep believing!

P.S. Perkins

CONVERSATIONS ABOUT COMMUNICATION: INWORD OUTWORD

CONVERSATION ONE: THE CHALLENGE

"Let's have a conversation. A conversation about Communication."

P.S.

Legacy is a word I think about a lot these days. Most of us come to this juncture during mid-life years, especially if we have children. I have a mother, a stepdad, brothers, a sister, and even older nieces and nephews starting to look at their legacy. What are they going to leave behind for the next generation? Many own homes, some are comfortably retired, savings, real estate, 401Ks, even researching 21st century investments like bitcoin in the Fourth Industrial Revolution we are all participating in, knowingly and unknowingly. However, my work and passion in the field of Human Communication, generated a new philosophy around legacy.

What is the most important thing I desire to leave behind? I have consumed and shared a lot of matter in this life, but after it's all said and done, what does matter matter? I determined after careful thought and observation, the most important legacy I could leave was **Language Legacy**™. The most important legacy anyone can leave behind is the legacy of cultivating right thoughts, words, emotions, and resultant behaviors so that our children and their children can create and maintain a life worth living and sharing. So, I began to have conversations about communication. As fate would have it, my discipline of study nourished my inspired vocation focusing on **Behavioral Communication** and its converging areas of study.

WORDS have power. My elders told stories as their elders told stories and the world around us is transfixed by the stories that continue to be perpetuated. They wanted us to believe in the stories they were told in hopes that "dreams do come true." However, the realities of life fostered a different story. Along with our ancestors, many of us feel as if we are "carrying the weight of the world on our shoulders." Is that how you feel at times? How about today? This moment? How do we cope with the burdens we feel in our everyday lives and relationships? We keep telling ourselves stories because they keep us going. Or do they?

As a child, I used to desire earnestly to twinkle my nose, wave a magic wand and end the confusion of the adults and companions around me. In part, that is what the fairytales were designed to do – build a fortress of illusion around us to help us cope with what the adults knew to be the inevitable – there was no tooth fairy, fairy godmother, nor any of the dozens of mythical creations planted in our minds to keep us moving towards somewhere over the rainbow. However, once the blinders are removed, once we stop drinking what I label the proverbial "cool-aid" of life, others label it the elixir of distractions, we wake to the reality that a fulfilling, productive, passionate life requires personal dedication. It is time to become self-aware to our complicity in refusing to do the tough work of maturing. Why? So, we can enjoy being alive to the personal journey of reclaiming self-knowledge and living a genuinely unique and fulfilling life! It is your gift from a universal mind capable of re-membering you back to your original purpose – to create a fulfilling life and gift it to others. I am inviting you to a conversation, a Conversation About Communication – YOUR communication.

"In the beginning was the word." John 1:1 Holy Bible, TLV

While no one of us holds the answers to the mysteries of the universe, the solution to world hunger, global wars, mass genocide...there is a world under our control. A place where our influence is so sovereign no-thing created on earth, above or below, can or desires to thwart our will. We all have free will to CHOOSE the course of our lives when allowed the opportunity through self-determination and the absence of social encumbrances. There is one supreme solution given to us all, and when given the faculties to do so, we can be victorious over the only world under our control – OURSELVES. Do you truly desire to experience happiness and self-fulfillment? Then you must AGREE to do so. You must come into mental, verbal, and physical agreement with your desires! The problem for all humankind is the inability to come to an understanding of how this can be done within the metaphysical realms of consciousness. **What is outward can only momentarily alter what is inward.** That is why we must go inward to change the influence of the outward. We have been provided with the solution that is available to all seeking, searching and finally arriving to a space of knowing. Knowing what?

Communication is synonymous with creation for humans

CONVERSATION TWO: THE REVELATION

Working as a Human Communication Practitioner has given me insight into how most of us so easily ignore the major solution to our consistently recycled personal and interpersonal problems. It is much easier to blame familial inadequacies, personal deficiencies, or societal factors for the daily upsets, setbacks, or lack of achievement in our own lives. We are all prone to look outside of ourselves for what ails us inside – the confusion, broken promises, unfulfilled dreams – we ALL have these experiences. However, mature in understanding the personal impact of these mental constructs impacting our daily outlook and perspective by examining a word that is our constant companion - **expectations.**

When I realized that I had turned the fairytales, social standards, and romance novels into sought after personal aspirations, it was very late in the game called "wake up!" I felt like a character in the movie The Matrix (1999), awakening from a long sleep designed to keep me complacent and compliant while unfulfilled, but satiated enough to go along. Which pill should I take - red or blue (movie reference)? Nothing was working out like the heroine in the Harlequin romance novels I read as a young girl. What happened? Did I take a detour? Did I not play my dealt cards correctly? I followed the rules as best I could as woman of color from an educated, middle-class Black family that achieved more than modest gains during and after Civil Rights. I graduated from "good" schools, chose an admirable profession, went to church, and believed in the adopted GOD of my resilient transatlantic ancestors...what was I doing wrong? PLENTY!

I learned my expectations had become prescriptions of how I should look, act, behave, and created a false belief system that IF I did it all according to the social engineers (who were also expecting their fairytale ending), all would turn out fabulous! My socially-prescribed expectations almost destroyed me – mind, body, and soul. Why? Because I kept looking outside of me to fix what was faltering inside of me. The "seed" that wanted desperately to be nourished could not be fed because I was too busy feeding social expectations allowed to take root and choke MY unique gifts and purpose. Understand, I had a checklist for everything and everybody: mother, father, sister, brother, friend, boyfriend, sister friend, education, politics, religion, happiness, beauty, duty...EVERYTHING! The script had already been written. I read it, memorized it, and played the only role I could play – FOLLOW! Most of us have even while feeling instinctually something is not right. Now, I am in no way diminishing nor disparaging personal goals or aspirations of "dreams come true"! I do believe in dreams, hopes and even miracles!

The question is WHAT are you aspiring towards? WHO do you believe is responsible for it? HOW do you propose to achieve it?

I had to let go of the expectation that cultural norms and expectations had the answer to MY journey, though they may provide viable ingredients to the roadmap, such as getting a degree. I had to realize that while my family and environment played a major role in my self-identity, I ultimately had to take ownership to navigate my future landscape. I had to dream THE dream that only I could and nurture it. Please listen with your heart to this important truth:

There is often a major discrepancy between our **aspirations** and our **inspiration.**

Very often, it is the aspiration that is the product of social prescriptions and expectations. Sometimes choosing our desired path is based on predetermined lineage or social status. Some are content and desiring to follow these paths and they should. However, too many find themselves caught up in the mistake of exchanging prescribed aspirations for their hearts desire and natural instincts/ gifts - inspiration. This is the plight of many desiring fulfillment but dying without it, internally and externally. I am convinced:

If we could ALL live, express and thrive WITHIN our inspiration, as opposed to being forced to acquire prescribed aspirations, there would be no human carnage of any sort.

Yes, that is my definition of a human utopia.

I had to learn some hard lessons:

1. It was no one else's job to make me happy or fulfilled or take me to the end of the rainbow.

2. I did not have the power to change others; support yes, change no.

3. No amount of replaying historical wrongs could make my present or future right or bright.

4. I needed to stop thinking everyone saw me as I wanted to or even deserved to be seen and reward me for it.

5. I needed to let everyone off the hook (expectations) realizing if they could do or could have done better, they would – even realizing that some would still choose not to.

6. Religion, though it can embody spiritual fulfillment, is not an intimate, trans-formative relationship with the Divine.

7. I AM whatever I say I AM. The "ownership statement" is the most important ones anyone will speak...the words following I AM _____.

These lessons, though a conscious part of my daily life, are not always adequately represented in my interactions with self and others. This level of maturity into ownership and self-responsibility is indeed a journey as wise teachers journeying a step ahead have shared. However, let me share an epiphany that propelled my journey forward and was gifted to me in the career I thought I chose, but most definitely chose me.

CONVERSATION THREE: MIND-FILLED

We appear to be careening into a world offering two divergent paths to the acquisition of human achievement. One path, more travelled, is one that is driven by the ambition to gain and consume at will and desire, no matter the consequence to human or earthly life. The blight of natural resources and the over-consumption of some continues to lead to the oppression and suffering of many. It is the dog-eat-dog path of survival of the fittest and many continue to travel it out of fear. It is a road filled with momentary satisfactions and thrills but too often monumental defeats devouring those caught in its web. It is based in a "HAVE, DO, BE" mentality.

The other path is encouraging the traveler to "awaken" to their mental prowess and embrace the uncharted neurological mindscape of human creative expansion – healing mind, body, and soul through harnessing the power of mental acuity. Human history is replete with the evolutionary findings of behavioral sociologist, neurological scientist, psychologist, cultural anthropologist, linguistic scientist, and others tapping into and unlocking the human potential. This is happening now more than anytime in human history especially with supportive nanotechnologies and AI intelligence.

An ancient and recent offering into the concept of self-awakening, is the belief system of **Mindfulness** used as a method of self-healing and personal empowerment. Seminars, workshops, and classes have become quite widespread and popular in organizational structures and institutions seeking to support the growth of clientele and personnel. However, this type of offering is generally reserved for those who are fortunate enough to work for or thrive in communities seeking "alternative" solutions to our personal and social ills. The practice seeks to teach and encourage its students to be aware of the present moment in a manner that allows them to make "mindful" choices and responses. But, for any method of mental and emotional ascension to become a practice, we must first move from a **mind-filled** to being able to BE consciously mindful. It is based in a "BE, DO, HAVE" philosophy.

You cannot have and keep what you are not!

I have worked in the arena of mindfulness for many years through the discipline of Human Communication recognized as the process of Intrapersonal Communication. It is designated as the first step of the Communication Staircase Model™, because it must be. Let us start at the beginning with a definition of Communication and the foundational role of Intrapersonal somewhat hidden within this definition.

"Communication happens whenever meaning is assigned to behaviors or the mental residue of behaviors."
(R. Zueschner, 2003, P.S. Perkins adapted)

Communication is a happening, but more than that, it should be an intentional, intellectual happening versus the biological ability to talk and hear. The mute do not talk, but they communicate. The deaf do not hear, but they listen. Sometimes during lectures or facilitation, I interject the phrase "Whose Listening?" This often startles my listeners and brings them back into the present. I then explain the use of the possessive, whose. Who is owning listening at this required moment? It is important to realize there is always at least two messages: the one sent by the encoder (creator) and the one received (decoder). We must OFTEN take the time to ask, "Did you hear what I think I said?"

When we are desiring a dialogue, we must not allow it to turn into what has been termed a duologue which can transpire into individuals talking over one another while consistently engaging with their own mental residue. To communicate effectively, we must control mental chatter that diverts from interacting with others. Remember:

The present (gift) is in the present (time) and it requires your presence (attentiveness)!

We must distinguish our talking from our communicating and our hearing from our listening by LEARNING how to do so. If we mimic communication like we mimic talking, well, I think the results are obvious.

When communicating, we engage in the function of **assigning meaning** to our and others **behaviors** (verbal and nonverbal) as a part of the cognitive processing necessary for survival. It is what we must do. Yet, it is the HOW we do it that determines all outcomes as well as the input from others whose HOW TO's can impact our own. We **assign** based on our individual enculturation processes. We select what we pay attention to based on what we are used to seeing, hearing, tasting, feeling, smelling. Our mental processes usually immediately reject the "foreign" clicking "delete" unless we give permission to proceed into the world of investigation to determine good or bad, friend or foe. Unfortunately, we often click delete too fast OR not fast enough (such as a culture we are wary of our baby investigating a wall socket)! Continuing, communication is often predetermined and dominated by **mental residue**. Residue? How does this component relate to communicating with self and others?

The process of enculturation creates the us we are. It begins in the developmental years and continues throughout life. It comes from the societal resources surrounding us. This is how we become the **mental residue** that creates our self-image, perspective, world view...our values, attitudes, and beliefs.

These memories and experiences become our internal noise – our self-talk – **our Intrapersonal Communication**. It is important to understand self-esteem, self-concept (worth), self- image and self-identity are ALL created within this process. It is where and how you live.

Notice the above diagram sharing the basic process of enculturation, including the way this process surfaces from the inner to the outer person sharing their values, attitudes, and beliefs. What is interesting to note is that by the time the inner communication processes come to the forefront of behavior, the individual has learned to wear the mask of socialization and show up as the presentational self – a concept often discussed in Intrapersonal and Interpersonal Communication. This is the self they think everyone expects to see and the roles everyone expects them to play. Below this is the perceived self – the individual they "wanna be", and lastly what I term the real self – desiring to come to the forefront of one's life.

Intrapersonal Communication competency is the ability to transform the mental residue into thoughts, words, patterns of thinking that produce your purpose and passion. It is also a competency that lets others off the proverbial hook and makes room for the residue reality that is theirs and theirs alone – you are no longer responsible unless you intentionally decide to be. It allows you to stop judging self and others but change what you can and want to change within **yourself.** It allows you to understand that you can make wiser decisions concerning whose residue you want to get into the mix with.

So, while I have a very healthy appreciation and adhere to some practices of mindfulness, the primary step to allowing such practices to move you towards a healthier life is to *"Be transformed by the re-NEW-ing of your mind"* (Holy Bible, TLV, emphasis mine). It is a communication process. Your thoughts, words, emotions, and resultant actions come from the internal noise constantly chattering within and it is here that you must begin to unpack the Intrapersonal disturbances that disrupt your mindfulness. The transformation we seek is an ongoing journey of examining, rooting out or modifying unwanted thoughts and patterns that we know are destructive to self and others. This must be intentional.

Did you know we all carry with us a contagion infecting and reinfecting ourselves and those around us all day long? We live in a world today where we must increasingly protect ourselves from viruses and pathogens that can be caught from one another, animals, the air we breathe, and the water we drink. How many of us have considered that we can have a clean bill of physical health and still make everyone around us sick; sometimes very sick? Yes, you are contagious every minute of the day. It is called emotional contagion. I will define it as the emotional energy we bring with us wherever we go. It affects the communication climate (temperature) of all our environments. The emotional energy can be either productive or nonproductive, uplifting or debilitating. You may not even be aware of it, but those around you are! "Oh, oh, here she comes!" Everyone is emotionally contagious. It is up to the individual to determine if they are spreading ease or dis-ease. Be positively contagious! LOVE! LIVE! LAUGH!

A word of caution: In my studies, I furthered this concept of emotional contagion into the "mind-field" of emotional transference. Be very watchful of those who are prone to intentionally transfer emotional states that are damaging to your mind, body, and soul. We all have days that are difficult to navigate; but there are some who thrive in negative states and as a result they infect those around them consistently. It is a habit, like a drug to them. Some people do not feel alive unless they are in a negative state. They have given control of their lives over to their feelings, inviting everyone around them to stay in their feelings. We ARE NOT our feelings. We use them, inviting and uninviting as useful. They are a tool of expression. Some are not aware of their condition. Maybe you can share this planner with them and begin their process of self-awareness and healing. Regardless, you must stop giving them permission to infect you and your environment unless it is to lift and seek solutions witnessing tangible progress!

"I am what I think I am. My thoughts are not separate from me."

Invite those you care about to the 30-day challenge of the Three-Selves Formula™ later in the chapter and all the other challenges in this Powerful Women Today Planner.

CONVERSATION FOUR: WORD UP!

We will spend the remaining conversations taking your **WORD UP!** Walking up the **Communication Staircase Model**™ (CSM) to examine how your Intrapersonal Communication is the primary factor impacting all communication experiences, not just with self, but others.

Seven (7) types of communication we engage in daily:

1. **Intrapersonal Communication** – Communication within oneself, mental residue

2. **Nonverbal Communication** – the conscious and/or subconscious sending and receiving of unspoken messages.

3. **Interpersonal Communication** – Dyadic exchange; communication between two

4. **Small Group Communication** – Comprised of 3 – 25 participants coming together for a common purpose

5. **Public Presentation** – Presenting before a captive audience

6. **Mass Communication** – Using media to persuade, inform, and entertain

7. **Intercultural Communication** – communication exchange that is altered due to differing cultural norms, attitudes, behaviors, beliefs.

Again, notice the first step of the model begins with you. As the model proceeds upward, each step encompasses a broader audience beyond steps one and two. The above model is not stagnant, but fluid communication exchanges that happen throughout our day. Within each of these communication arenas reside concepts, formulas, tools of expertise and function. Human Communication is a discipline that must be learned through the intellect; otherwise, all we do is mimic without pragmatic comprehension, which is a true recipe for personal danger and generational misfortunes.

Think about the day you just began or finished or are half-way through. How many of these communication experiences have you had? So far, at least one, Intrapersonal and possibly two, Nonverbal because you are probably dressed. It starts with that "wake up" self-talk. How many of us remember the adage "getting up on the wrong side of the bed?" I often ask my audiences to explain what that means. It is interesting to watch individuals go into their mental residue to pull forth the explanation. It is also interesting to note, most say, "I never thought about the meaning, but I always understood what was meant. Someone woke up in a bad mood."

As you wake, your mind immediately begins the process of reacquainting you to the world in your recent memory and the world around you. For most of us, that involves laying still for a moment while allowing a flood gate of thoughts and feelings to come to the forefront of our awareness. Dreams, last night's argument, the movie you fell asleep on, the days work ahead, an important task...it is all there vying for your attention. As you wake completely and ready for your day, you are ALREADY on one side of the bed or the other! And now it is time to climb the stairs! Did you leave that mood, those thoughts, that energy behind? As you went into the bathroom, kitchen, car, public transportation, office, factory, grocery store, did you leave you behind? Of course not! Why? This is where the three-selves method of thought-transformation offers much needed support to mitigate the constant "other" realities that we interact with.

"YOU take YOU wherever YOU go!"

CONVERSATION FIVE: DID YOU HEAR WHAT I THINK I SAID?

Let us enter the world of Ashley, a Powerful Woman Today, as she goes up and down the Communication Staircase during her usual day as a professional, wife, mother, and manager. Notice her thought process as she engages with the practice of the **Three-selve**s to navigate the delicate and sometimes difficult communication experiences she encounters. And this is just ONE DAY!

COMMUNICATION STAIRCASE MODEL APPLIED

Intrapersonal Awakening

"Huh! What time is it?" Glancing at the clock, Ashley sees it's only 6:00 AM and she can probably doze another 30 minutes, but hearing a noise from the kitchen, she becomes wide awake. Her husband remains sound asleep as she handles the 7-year-olds attempt at making breakfast for the family. Cute, but not today!

Nonverbal Communication

Having spent an unplanned 45-minutes cleaning up a mess her 7-year-old made trying to fix breakfast for the family, Ashley quickly rushes back to the bedroom to quickly dress (Time is the nonverbal arena called Chronemics) as she opens her closet to hurriedly choose an outfit to wear for a day filled with meetings she must preside over (Appearance is nonverbal communication). She wants to look her best and feels anxious after her abrupt morning start. Her husband is taking a longer than usual shower and she did not have time for her morning tea!

Notice, Ashley is becoming mind-filled with the morning's unexpected delays.

Interpersonal Communication

Ashley's husband bounces out of the bathroom looking ready, bright, and perky, and she can feel herself getting more irritated. Her husband tries to kiss her as she quickly brushes past him to the shower.

Insight: Appropriate and truthful self-disclosure is a vital road to intimacy.

We all seek into-me-see.

Driving to work, she has a minute to reflect on her morning, acknowledging it was not a good start, and she turns on soothing music to try and hit restart. Then she hits traffic! What next!

As Ashley arrives at the office, her administrative assistant lets her know the team, including the boss, has been waiting 15 minutes.

Because Ashley is still thinking about the difficulties of her morning and rushing in, she brusquely asks her assistant for the meeting documents and rushes into the meeting. This sets a tone between her and the Admin for the rest of the day.

Small Group

Though Ashley tried hard to regroup, the meeting did not go as smoothly as she hoped. She felt put on the spot by one colleague who kept asking for updates that were not available and started to feel attacked. She had prepared well and did not understand why things were not going as planned. The meeting adjourned early without the consent needed to move the project forward.

Ashley did not feel her usual confident self, and this was just the beginning of a long day. She needed to regroup before her board presentation that afternoon.

Public Presentation

This area does not require an auditorium of people, nor is it just about "public speaking". It is the opportunity to capture the attention of small or large groups in any setting, using any device that offers information, persuasion, or entertainment (the three types of communicating). Ashley was looking forward to addressing the company board about the progress of her division but her early morning "wake up" and workplace meeting daunted her confidence and energy. She digs deep to muster up the confidence through her Nonverbal presence as she walks confidently into the room. She remembers an important tool: eye contact with all participants BEFORE engaging! This supports her ability to capture the attention of her audience and take control of the communication environment.

Mass Communication

After the meeting that went much better than the morning, Ashley felt she had regained some of her footing and was able to knockout several pressing items, including making sure she sent an email, cc'ing her boss, and requesting the updates asked for in the morning meeting. She even set up a virtual meeting with the children's school counselors since progress reports would be coming home soon. Ashley does her best to stay highly functioning in the ever-increasing digital world and its demands.

Intercultural Communication

It had been a busy day of interaction and making sure the necessary tasks were completed. There had been no time to catch up with her Administrative Assistant, Min. However, before leaving work, Ashley realizes there is one more important communication item to take care of – smooth things out with Min. Min shared with her that her Chinese name meant "sensitive or soft-hearted". Indeed, Min was always available to listen and offer consultation but only when asked. Ashley began to explore Chinese culture when she hired Min and learned a little about the culture's conflict management style of face-saving. Intercultural competency must be a major focus of the global workforce and an inclusive society where increasingly we are all interdependent. Intercultural Communication competency can be measured as a pinnacle of workplace and societal success.

Ashley understood Min's conflict management style was different from her own and as a result, Min remained quiet most of the day after the brusque morning exchange with Ashley. Ashley reflected that Min would never think to confront her in a manner deemed culturally disrespectful, nor would she bring up an interpersonal matter during such a hectic day. Min has become much more vocal about her concerns as Ashley requested. So, after complimenting Min on really supporting her efforts to get on top of the details of the day, Ashley apologized for her earlier behavior and asked if Min had any questions or concerns, she wanted to go over. They parted with ease and reassurance for a productive tomorrow.

Intrapersonal Reclamation

As Ashley drove home, she reflected on her day and the way she mentally and emotionally reacted internally and externally. She understands the InWORD OutWORD dynamics of effective communication and continues to engage in the daily process of self-monitoring, self-reflecting and self-adjusting. It is making her life more peaceful, intentional, and inclusive. It is a daily struggle with her mental residue, but she is willing to do the work and assured VICTORY. As she drives home to her residence, in heavy traffic and blaring horns, she turns up her mental volume and meditates on her current emotional energy to bring forward the smile at the front door. She truly realizes:

We are ALL residents of our residue!

Ashley's next thought? "Now, it's time for the   real challenge of the day! What's for dinner?

What the heck! Take out, and I know just the place where there is something for everybody!"

References

Perkins, P.S. (2008). The Art and Science of Communication: Tools for Effective Communication in the Workplace. New Jersey: John Wiley and Sons, Inc.

Graphic Designers, P.S. Perkins, Emilio Lee, 2008, Colleen Bent Technologies, 2021

Mel H. Abraham. (n.d.). Thoughtpreneurs Academy. Retrieved March 19, 2021, from https://www.melabrahamtraining.com/

Society., S. M. (2016). Holy Bible, Tree of Life Version (TLV). Grand Rapids: Baker Books.

Wachowski, L., Wachowski, L., Wachowski, L., Wachowski, L., Silver, J., Davis, D., . . . Ping, Y. W. (Writers), & Paterson, O. (Producer). (1999). The matrix [Video file].

Zeuschner, R. F. (2003). Communicating today: The essentials. Boston: Allyn and Bacon.

30 Day Challenge

BENEFIT

You are now challenging yourself to live a healthier, smarter, and more productive life. You already know WORDS MATTER! You have just read the chapter **Conversations About Communication: InWORD OutWORD** and now it is time to engage the real you versus the **presenting-self** (how you show up) on a journey of thought and emotion exploration. We are not always in charge of the thoughts that circulate through the atmosphere and "drop" into unaware minds. As thoughtpreneurs (Mel Abraham, 2010) we can no longer afford to downplay the fact that: **thoughts** become **words** and **emotions** which become **behaviors** which become **habits** which become the character of **who we are** to ourselves and others!

This 30-day exercise CHALLENGES YOU to take control of your thought-life in a manner that requires you knowingly determine the words and emotions you thrive in daily. It is a process that requires you spend time becoming aware of your **rumination patterns** (thinking certain thoughts repeatedly). Moving beyond the bio-physical mechanics of language acquisition and usage, you are encouraged to examine the areas of **metacognition** and **metacommunication** – the abilities to examine how we process thoughts/feelings, and the resultant communication (behaviors). Thinking about what you are thinking about. Communicating about how you are communicating, with self and others.

> *We are all materializing the world around us through our thoughts, words and deeds. Some are doing it intentionally and some are not.*

Our collective 30-day challenge is to engage in the Personal-Thought-Development exercise entitled **"The Three-Selves."** As the number indicates, this exercise entails three phases of involvement:

THE 3 SELVES

Self-Monitor   *Self-Reflect*   *Self-Adjust*

You desire a change in all areas of your life. The tool of the **Three-Selves** will support this, period. It is an InWORD OutWORD reality.

Powerful Women Today™ is empowering women all over the world with our **Eight (8) Pillars of Wellness and Success**. The only way to achieve these tools of personal, social, professional, and spiritual development, is to engage our WORD, powerfully aligning with the pillars!

Your **Intrapersonal Communication** competency will:

1. **Physically** ensure that you are thinking and speaking health.
2. Support your efforts to be **Socially** adept around others.
3. Help you monitor your **Emotions** as you move into the truth that you are not your feelings, but they are yours to use, enjoy, and control. No longer being controlled by the need to be needed.

4. Bring greater awareness to your **Occupational** spaces understanding that YOU take YOU wherever YOU go!

5. Lift your **Financial** discussions about wealth from a "poverty, never enough" mentality to a channel of giving as well as receiving.

6. Bring to the forefront of ALL areas of your life, the **Spiritual** truth "As she thinks within herself, so is she." Proverbs 23:7, Holy Bible, TLV

7. Help you gain **Intellectual** wisdom that all knowledge comes from outside in. Eat wisely.

8. Assist you in walking in **Environmental** consciousness filled with gratitude and respect for the earth that sustains us.

CHALLENGE

TOOLS NEEDED: A Journaling Process and Determination to be VICTORIOUS!

Our collective 30-day challenge is to engage in the Personal-Thought-Development exercise entitled **"The Three-Selves."** As the number indicates, this exercise entails three phases of involvement:

1. **Self-monitoring** = Check in with your emotions at any given time of the day AND "catch a thought - EXAMINE IT!

2. **Self-reflecting** = Immediately upon catching that thought, spend whatever time you need or have reflecting on its health – its outcome as far as you can see.

3. **Self-adjusting** = The final step is to ADJUST. Make a clear, careful decision to allow the thought to proceed because you are assured in your mind, body, and soul, YOU CAN LIVE WITH ITS RESULTS! If not, CLICK DELETE

and most important, REPLACE the unwanted thought with a new thought, act, or deed that nullifies the potency of the thought/feeling.

I am inviting you to this 30-day challenge as a BEGINNING of a life transformation of your relationship with WORDS. Some of these thoughts/words have been living within the dendrite regions of your mind for days, months, years, waiting for the "right" conditions to resurface and create havoc (or peace) in your mental space, which in turn becomes your eternal space – InWORD OutWORD! You will do this in an effort to replace toxic, debilitating thoughts with renewed perspectives of hope and competence.

SAMPLE JOURNALING PATTERN

Write down the thought or pattern of thinking using this (or a preferred) reflective writing pattern:

THREE-SELVES REFLECTIVE JOURNALING PATTERN

1. Catch the thought/thought-pattern. **Self-monitoring**
2. What is your emotional state of being at that exact moment? **Self-monitoring**
3. Time and day of the week? **Self-reflecting**
4. Who you are in the company of (alone, family, spouse, friend, co-workers)? **Self-reflecting**
5. Location where thought(s) occurred (home, work, shopping, lunch)? **Self-reflecting**

6. Your internal reaction/response to your awareness
   of the thought?   *Self-reflecting*

7. Determine if you desire to experience the outcome of
   this behavior? *Self-adjusting*

8. The resulting action concerning the thought (continue, delete, invite,
   uninvite)? *Self-adjusting*

9. Upon going to bed or waking, re-member to acknowledge your progress
   and BEGIN ANEW!

The challenge takes time, but isn't that why it is called a journey? I am not saying go around with your head buried in your Reflection Journal all day, but as you catch the thought, put it in your phone, jot a note on the back of a bill/letter, shopping list...anywhere that is easily accessible...THEN, when in the quiet of your "midnight hour" go back and retrieve the most energizing OR the most troubling, and use the reflective pattern to investigate the ROOT causes of these positive or negative infiltrators.

No one can think or speak to create your life for you!

Results? YES! I would not have spent 20 plus years creating, using, refining, and sharing this formula if I thought for one minute it would not support your efforts – anyone's efforts!

30-days to shift your awareness of thoughts meant to keep you filled with self-pity, destroy relationships, lose your mind readjusting to thoughts that build dreams! During your 30-day challenge to InWORD health, watch your OutWORD experiences start to become a reflection of what you now KNOW is possible –

mastery over the thoughts, emotions, words - behaviors that have taken control over you - mind over matter instead of matter over mind! You will not only feel a change but experience a change in your ability to call forward emotions that are facilitating instead of debilitating!

Lastly, EVERY day is the possibility of a new start...every day you engage in monitoring, reflecting upon, and adjusting just **one** thought, is one thought closer to your personal freedom and victory over the uninvited energies creating a life you do not want to continue to live in. Instead of being an extra in your own movie, BECOME THE STAR! Oh, and BTW...it's never too early to hand this legacy down to your children and family to lift their **WORD UP**!

About the Author

P.S. Perkins is the Founder and Senior Consultant of the Human Communication Institute (www.hci-global.com) and currently is an award-winning Instructor of Human Communication at the University of the District of Columbia and Prince George's Community College. An alumnus of UNC-Chapel Hill (BA) and New York University (MA), P.S. is the author of the highly acclaimed business self-help book, The Art and Science of Communication: Tools for Effective Communication in the Workplace, by John Wiley & Sons, Inc., e-book 77 Best Way to Communicate in 7 Steps, as well as a contributing author to the books Laws of Communication, Literary Anthologies' Hallelujah Anyhow and SURVIVAL P.L.A.N.S., World Healing

World Peace Poetry Anthology vol. 2. and Wake Up Women. Additionally, P.S. writes articles on Human Communication as well as Short Stories/Poetry/Prose for a variety of journals, magazines, and community sources. As a Motivational Speaker and Behavioral and Intercultural Communication Training Specialist, P.S. offers presentations, lectures, and workshops on a myriad of Communication topics including: Cultural Sensitivity and Inclusion, Civic Communication and Community Policing, Adult and Youth Behavioral Communication, Leadership Communication, Interpersonal Relationship Maintenance, Workplace Communication, Language Legacy, and the Performing and Communication Arts.

P.S. Be true to your word because it will always be true to you!

Contact Information
P. S. Perkins, Founder and CCO
Company: Human Communication Institute
Email: psp@hci-global.com
LinkedIn: www.linkedin.com/in/pamela-p-s-perkins-80a60711
Facebook: www.facebook.com/psperkins1
Website: www.hci-global.com

Dedication

I dedicate this book to the four greatest loves of my life:

My soulmate and husband Jeremy, and our three beautiful, spirited sons.

I love you all 'big and lots', 'to the moon and back' and no matter what.

Hailey Patry

LIFE LESSONS

From an exuberantly happily married mom of three boys, international speaker to over a million audience members, best-selling and award winning author... who once was a girl that battled 8 years of depression and anorexia, overcame two suicide attempts as a teen, survived a violent rape, escaped domestic violence, and finally found happiness in her 30's, including a second marriage to her soul mate.

If my life could work out this well, after everything I have gone through... yours can too.

Instead of writing you a regular book chapter, I asked myself: "What is the most meaningful thing I could share with you, the reader, the amazing woman who bought this planner, such that, your life would go up from here?" I decided the most valuable thing I could share with you, is a bountiful, juicy list of my best tips, my personal practices and what I've learned from the trenches of life, love and business. Instead of a cohesive story, you're about to dive into 52 Life Lessons that I hope you will use to avoid making the costly mistakes I made, to help you travel more safely on your journey to happiness, love and success, and to go out and make this year one of your best years yet. I believe in you! Use these nuggets, some old and some new, to guide you. And remember, if you are ever lost, stuck or really afraid of what comes next... you are not alone. I am here for you and just a text message away.

I have divided the life lessons into three categories, which include YOUR HAPPINESS, YOUR RELATIONSHIP and YOUR SUCCESS. You will notice that there are far more lessons about your personal happiness than the other two areas, and that was intentional. You see, YOU are the common theme in your life. A mentor once said to me: "wherever YOU go, there YOU will be". You bring your personal issues into your work and into your relationships. So, if you are the key domino, that influences every other area of your life...well then, let's support you first. Once you get to the 30 day challenge I have created for you in this planner, you will see that it's all about being your best self.

Alright, deep breath, here goes a lifetime of learning, condensed to my favorites at this time. (Written at the one year mark of the global pandemic in March 2021.) Enjoy!

LIFE LESSONS FOR YOUR HAPPINESS

1. How we allocate our precious 5 resources determines the quality of our lives. Those resources include Time, Energy, Money, Attention and Intention. Attention – where your eyes, ears and mind wander to. Intention – what you set your mind to. Intention is a very powerful thing. Use it wisely. I set intentions for my mood, behavior and outcomes. Be intentional, set great intentions, and wonderful results and experiences will be more likely to follow.

2. More important to note than the fact that days have 24 hours, is that a week has 168 hours. Using your 168 hours intentionally, by design, and very carefully,is ultimately the reality you live every week. How you spend your time in life, ultimately makes up your life.

3. Scheduling your life makes a massive difference to how much you like your life. It also equips you with the ability to clearly know when to say yes and when to say no, when other people are requesting your time or making invitations. Here is the order in which I schedule my life, now that my life is fabulous: time for self, time for connection, time for joy, time for work, white space on my calendar, and lastly, chores and responsibilities that I may need to hire out for or delegate to someone else.

4. Your self-worth mirrors your standards for everything in your life: Friends, earnings, environment and surroundings, relationships, how you allow yourself to be treated, whether you stand for anything and what you stand

for, your assertion or passiveness, your confidence, your thoughts, beliefs, intentions, actions, results and outcomes.

5. Raising your self-worth so you know you are a 10 out of 10, 100% worthy of love, affection, abundance, happiness and greatness,is one of the most important projects to commit to in your lifetime. It is never too late to raise your self-worth and heal from your past, AND it is never too soon to start the journey to worthiness.

6. Trauma leads to gifts and blessings after you heal. The key is to find your blessings in the messes that have come into your life, and then choose how you will bounce,don't bounce back,bounce better! For example, overcoming my rape and depression are keys to me being able to help my clients as quickly as I do. The gifts from what I went through include empathy, compassion, understanding and helping my clients feel safe to share their darkest experiences with me, so thentogether, I can help them heal. Living through 30 years of trauma, and not receiving the right help became a blessing in my life because I developed the tools that I needed to heal and thrive, and now I can share those tools with others who need them. So, what are the blessings from the messes of your life? How can you turn your most challenging experiences into growth and positive outcomes?

7. Forgiveness is possible for ALL things, and it's an act of kindness for you, not for the person or event you are forgiving. In the grand scheme of things, everything becomes perfect when you realize your life is happening for you and not to you. AND, every challenge you have ever faced, came into your life to MAKE you and NOT to break you. As a Master Coach in Radical Living and Radical Forgiveness, this is something I deal with a lot. I get it. Forgiveness can feel so hard, it can even feel impossible, especially when you know that what happened was not okay, perhaps not even legal.

The truth is, when you create your life from this present moment and forward to be a life that you love so much,you will see in hindsight that every moment leading you to this one had to happen as it did for you to arrive here. And if you have come to a place in your life where you deeply love yourself, your reality, your gifts,well then it would seem true that everything that led you here was necessary. Ultimately, you would no longer have parts of your life you'd wish to erase, and that is the magic of forgiveness. In the end, when you do the work (and I can certainly help you with this), there is nothing wrong anymore, and nothing left to forgive. I would not take back my rape, for I am grateful that I had to go through whatever I had to go through to become who I am now, to do what I do now, and to contribute to this world the way I do. Everything I do and everyone I help would not be possible without my past experiences.

8. Scars are beautiful. Victimhood is not. You can be victorious, a champion of your life, proud of your battles, your scars, your learnings, your growth, your whole story. Own your story, tell it proudly, make something beautiful out of your life and inspire others to share their story too.

9. Nature is so crucial. The amount of time you spend outside (that is, if you enjoy being outside) dramatically impacts your mental health and wellbeing. I choose to be outside a minimum of three hours a day, even when it is freezing in our Canadian winters. Dress for the elements of your climate and go soak up the bounty of your trails, parks, beaches, forests...whatever calls you.

10. Goals are weak. Promises are much stronger. In order to design and then achieve your best year ever, you'll want to set goals to honor a balanced life. In my signature workshop and annual planning class called "Designing Your Best Year Ever", we start by replacing the word goal with promise, and shift your relationship to the things you say you want to do, become, experience or achieve in a year. Next, we set intentions for your self-care and celebration, connection and relationships, uncluttering your life and dealing with mess. Then we focus on up-levelling with learning and personal growth, breakthrough goals that support you in claiming new ways of being for the coming year (which by the way can start anytime, and does

not need to begin on January 1st), and of course, we set an abundance goal around your finances, your career, business, investments, etc.

11. If you are serious about what you want to do, become, experience, or achieve in a year, then you'll need to make a proper action plan, which is something I love helping my clients with. Start with the end in mind and work it backwards. Figure out where you need to be at, progress wise, at each quarter point in the year. For the first quarter, figure out where you need to be each month. For the first month, decide where you need to be each week. And for the very first week, plan out exactly what you need to do on a daily basis and get those items scheduled properly into your chosen calendar system.

12. Let's talk about habits. Your collection of habits, for better or for worse, dramatically impact the quality of your life in all areas. It's not just choosing which habits you want to make, break or tweak, it's about what kind of person you want to become. For example, are you wanting to be someone whose word is golden, has incredible follow through, has amazing sleep hygiene, pristine oral health, optimal vitality from the best food, hydration, rest and movement? Someone who has positive self-talk and mental health, pampers yourself with care, has healthy relationships and friendships, and a solid relationship with money? Are you wanting to be a morning person, hold a plank for 5 minutes, have impeccable cardio-vascular health? Are you wanting to become calm, mindful, present and conscious? You must first decide who you want to become and then figure out which habits will support you in becoming that person...that upgraded version of YOU!

13. Habits won't form or break by accident. It takes a lot to form a great habit or break a non-supportive habit, so once you have set yourself in motion, don't break your stride. 3 cycles of 21 days are a great place to start when planning to create a new habit. Also, rather than break a bad habit, think of which new habit you will replace it with. For example, I am a chocolate person. When I am sad, mad, stressed, hurt, or insert any other challenging emotion of your choosing, I want chocolate. So, instead of saying to

myself "Hailey, stop eating chocolate as an emotional eating vice" I created a new habit: Do a 5 minute stretch, drink 8-16 ounces of water, and check in with myself if I still feel I NEED chocolate, or notice how my need for it dulled down to a want, which I can choose not to give into, or perhaps the craving went away all together.

14. Treat yourself like a great coach would. When you're injured or unwell... DO NOT FORCE YOURSELF to keep on keeping on. Hit the bench, see the trainer, get the massage, do the physio, eat the best recovery food, rest and get better. Be in peak shape when you return to play this game of life. At the same time, do not accept laziness, excuses and self-doubt. Lovingly push yourself (when you are well) to do and to be the best you can be. It's like working out alone versus with a trainer. With a trainer you will always complete more repetitions than when you are alone, and your form will be better and safer. So, treat yourself like the best coach and trainer would. Value yourself like a pro athlete, honor your health and your body, rest and repair from your life as needed, and when you are well, give it your very best, like your coach's voice is ringing in your mind letting you know how much they believe in you, know you can do it, and are right there with you cheering you on and waiting to celebrate you. It sounds confusing to know when to push yourself harder and when to rest and recover... but it's simple actually. It's about learning the difference for yourself of when you are well versus unwell and in need of TLC.

15. Ask questions. Do not make yourself small, silent or invisible. If you are in a class, participate. If you have a question, ask it. If you need something before you can move into massive action, get it looked after. A silent and stuck version of you does no one any favors. Become an ASK-Hole. Just because you ask for things in life does not guarantee that you will get everything you have asked for, but I guarantee you will get more than the person who was afraid to ask at all.

16. Be assertive. It is the best way to be. Not passive, not aggressive, and not passive aggressive. Be assertive! And if you struggle with this, you deserve

coaching and support to become the most confident and calm, assertive version of yourself. And in case you were wondering, yes, even shy people can become assertive. I used to be so shy I ate my lunch in the bathroom in high school. Now I can speak to crowds of over 25,000 people. It was a choice to become self-expressed and assertive, one I worked on and you can learn how to make the shift too.

17. Self-advocate, especially around your health. Stand for the best care possible. Do your research, be in the know, ask for the tests you want, and don't accept less than the best care for yourself. You are worth it and quite literally, sometimes your life depends on it. I have been close to death more than once, and I learned a lot from those experiences. Be an "ask-hole" when it comes to your health too!

18. As people, we are "carrot-minded". We need things to look forward to. One of my favourite ways to keep depression at bay, is to constantly play a game with my own mind, where I declare what I have to look forward to. Every evening, I choose what I can look forward to in the morning. Every morning I choose what to look forward to for the evening. Every Monday I choose what to look forward to for the weekend, and so on. This keeps me focussed on infusing moments of joy, fun, adventure and connection into my schedule, so that I can get through the tougher parts of the day or the week, with a hopeful countdown to the next great thing.

19. Eliminate overwhelming and rolling to do lists. Consider using a system to support you, such as my system called "My AI,I" which I am happy to share with you on your free, first coaching call. When you go to bed every evening feeling like an overwhelmed failure because there are so many items still left undone on your to-do list, you can't help but have anxious thoughts, high stress and lower self worth. Stop the cycle. Take everything on your list and either put in the time to complete it, as an appointment on your calendar, or put it on a list you'll review monthly or a list you'll review yearly. Every night you deserve to hit the pillow feeling complete, proud

and accomplished. And all you need to finish are today's tasks. The rest have a time and a place.

20. Have more experiences than stuff.

21. Have more joy and less obsessive perfection.

22. Let the house be a mess if it needs to be, so you can focus on the needs of the hearts who live in your home, yours included.

23. Take inventory of your happiness in each of the key areas I've noted below, and rate them once a month. Then choose which areas to focus on each month with extra TLC. For each area below score yourself out of 10for how happy you are with this area of your life. Then answer the following questions for any area you want to improve:

   ☐ How is it now?

   ☐ How Would I rather it be?

   ☐ What can be done about it?

   ☐ What will I do about it in the next 24 hours?

   ☐ Do I need to enlist help? If so, who? And when will I contact them?

Personal Happiness Areas:

☐ Health/Body

☐ Mental Health

☐ Sleep

☐ Energy/Vibration

☐ Personal Growth

☐ Finances

☐ Business/Career

☐ Fun and Adventure

☐ Home Life and Location

☐ Romance/Love/Passion

☐ Family and Friends

24. Nourish yourself properly. The quality and quantity of what you put past your lips, affects every single cell in your body, as well as your energy, mood, brain clarity, mobility, vitality, inflammation/pain levels, libido, appearance, digestion, confidence, life expectancy and so much more.

25. Hydrate properly. The formula I use for how much water to consume is my weight in pounds, divided in 2, and that is the number of ounces I need, not including extra water for exercise. (For example. 140 pounds divided by 2 = 70 ounces)

26. Rest up. Sleep and feeling rested affects every area of your life, including how well you are able to earn money, relate to others, manage your mood, your physical health and so much more. It is crucial to having a great life. Plan restoration breaks into your day for optimal performance AND well-being. Plan your sleep and wake cycle and remember that good sleep hygiene matters a lot too.

27. Movement matters and is such a key part of a healthy and happy life. (More on this in the challenge.) There are many forms of movement that can be beneficial depending on the state of your health and your goals. Work with a professional to help you decide what movement mix is best for you each week, but at the very least, if you are able to walk and stretch, put these two activities into your daily schedule. Your body and mind will thank you for it.

28. Your mindset, mood and outlook are pliable. You can choose to improve them and there are specific tools, skills, habits, rituals and routines that support better emotional health and wellbeing. Really, it all starts with you acknowledging how ideal your current mindset, mood and outlook are, deciding if you would like to improve any of them, and believing that you are worthy and capable. You may need professional help to achieve the MMO (mindset, mood and outlook) you desire. I can help.

29. Visualization, stillness, silence, meditation, prayer, what ever works for you to set your best mindset in motion – start your days with this before you turn on your phone and start checking notifications. And end your days with your chosen modality for a peaceful close to the day.

    My personal regimen before bed is to say my affirmations mantra, visualize the amazing tomorrow that I intend to create, and press play on my fave guided meditation for sleep with my phone far away and on airplane mode.

    You can choose to answer this question before bed, or once you wake up: My dream outcome for the day is???

    And finally, set your promised plan in motion, either before bed or when you wake up:

    a. What is my most important action to take for each of my 3 happiness/life projects?

    b. What are the ways of being I need to step into, to support my success on my happiness/life projects?

30. The reader/author in you has a craving to be acknowledged. A good life has pages in it. Pages you read, pages you write, pages you reflect on, plan on, schedule on. A great life is lived on purpose and reading/writing are part of taking in supportive content that aligns with your life goals and promises, as well as putting out supportive content, whether it is private, for your eyes only, or public to inspire others. What beneficial content will you read today? What will you write today? A journal entry, gratitude, your daily plan, poetry, a promise, a letter to a loved one, an apology, an item on your bucket list?

31. Be a productivity goddess – get the things done that you have been putting off but know you will be so happy once they're complete. Can you spend even 10 minutes a day knocking something off your list, or tackling

just 10 minutes of a bigger project, so you feel that whoosh of pride and accomplishment?

32. Take stock of your life in all areas: your happiness, your relationships, your career - and after knowing what your starting place is, then picking your ideal destination/outcome, you can begin to make your plans. Just like Google Maps, you will need to know your starting point, destination, and things that can get in your way, like traffic, construction, and accidents. It's similar for your life. You can work with a coach of your choice, someone like me, to help you spot what could be holding you back and getting in your way. There are things in your blind spot, and you can't solve what you can't see.

LIFE LESSONS FOR YOUR RELATIONSHIP

1. We choose our significant others to be a match for our self-worth at the time.

2. True love exists. You have to first know you are worthy and deserving, and then design the love you want to call into your life. But... love and relationships are hard when you don't have the skills to be a happy couple. Learning my 5 Step I.D.E.A.L. Love Method, and my 6 Skills of Happy Couples, will help you succeed at loving happily ever after. Here are the skills you'll want to master:

    ▢ Discover how to start loving each other the "right" way and quickly fill your hearts with love again.

    ▢ Gain instant reconnection by mastering the simple art of Heart-to-Heart conversations.

    ▢ Learn how easy it can be, to finally have everything you want in your relationship - well, almost everything, with loving negotiations.

    ▢ Discover the number one tool to alleviate stress and tension with your partner, with meaningful apologies.

☐ Date each other and fall in love again by using quality time wisely.

☐ Reignite your love and passion to beat the odds with a happy, healthy, fun, and - yes - lasting relationship.

3. Take inventory of your happiness in each of the key areas I've noted below, and rate them once a month. Then choose which areas to focus on each month with extra TLC. For each area below, score yourself out of 10 for how happy you are with this area of your relationship. Then answer the following questions for any area you want to improve:

☐ How is it now?

☐ How Would I rather it be?

☐ What can be done about it?

☐ What will we do about it in the next 24 hours?

☐ Do we need to enlist help? If so, who? And when will we contact them?

The relationship areas:

☐ Appreciation

☐ Respect

☐ Trust

☐ Forgiveness/Peace

☐ Resiliency

☐ Love and Kindness

☐ Sex

☐ Intimacy/Romance

☐ Communication

☐ Fun and Adventure

☐ Finances

[] Parenting (if applicable) or Family Values

[] Spousal Health

[] Attraction

[] Division of Labour

4. Have you ever sat across from your partner and wondered, during the awkward silence, what you could possibly say to make things better? Many couples feel like they have lost their words, their conversation skills and even the confidence to communicate at all... because they feel stuck.

    Good news, there is a conversation formula that works to improve your connection and fulfillment, if you do the work. This is the very same heart-to-heart conversation formula I have used with all of my private clients as they restored, rewrote and enhanced their relationships. It's amazing how much you can accomplish with this one conversation.

    Take some time to plan what you are going to say, schedule the time and have this talk. Here's the formula to bring you and your partner closer together again, with a good heart-to-heart chat:

    [] My vision for our relationship is...

    [] The apology I want to make to you are...

    [] The request I have of you is...

5. There are many relationships that can heal after infidelity. But long before I will help a couple heal, I have six conditions that must be met in order to take them on. If these conditions are not met, I don't feel confident that their relationship will recover or that it should be recovered.

    Conditions and prerequisites for a marriage or relationship to have a good chance of healing after infidelity:

- The one who cheated is remorseful.

- The one who cheated takes full ownership for their actions.

- The one who cheated has cut off contact with whomever they engaged with in adultery.

- The one who cheated is willing to give full disclosure and access to proof of information to their partner.

- The partner who was cheated on is willing to look at what their part might have been in co-creating the condition that existed before the infidelity.

- Both partners still want to be together and to work on their relationship, getting professional help.

6. If you want to receive meaningful apologies, it's time to learn how to give a meaningful apology. This simple formula was taught to me by one of my mentors, and it is life-changing! It allows you to clean up relationship messes quickly and stop fighting about the same things repeatedly, if of course you take it seriously and keep your commitments.

   Here is the framework to make things right when you've messed up:

   - What I want to clean up with you is...

   - The impact on you is...

   - The impact on me is...

   - What you can count on me for from now on is...

7. Weekly dates are like oxygen for your relationship. Studies show that couples who date each other at least once a week, are 3.5 times happier. Spend quality time together and make it special.

8. It takes one before it takes two. Be your best self and your truest most authentic self. Work on being whole and complete within your self and don't expect your partner to fill up your emptiness. Your happiness is your job.

9. And a few final tips... Have tons of fun as a couple, make lots of memories together, and touch as often as you can. Not everyone is fortunate enough to have someone in their life to hold. If you love someone, let them know and show them with your words and actions.

LIFE LESSONS FOR YOUR SUCCESS

I will keep these brief because so much depends on what industry you are in. I welcome you to schedule a complimentary coaching session with me if you want to explore more about these concepts for your business.

1. Increase your "Earnability", which is the amount of money you can generate in an hour, so you can spend less time working and more time living your life. Plus, always remember that happiness pays and unhappiness costs. Clients love to work with happy professionals.

2. Workshops are an amazing way for the public to experience you in a safe format and want more of what you teach. I love helping my clients create workshops that convert attendees to raving fans.

3. Your sample experience must be stellar! When potential clients first get a taste of what you do, make sure you wow them with an impeccable and memorable experience that leaves them ready to purchase your offer. Be professional, prepared, caring and most importantly, deliver real value.

4. Networking is a learnable skill and something I love to teach. If your networking skills don't land you multiple appointments from every event you attend, let's fix that for you.

5. Sharing your story is brave, generous and smart. It lets your audience connect with you, feel safe with you and be inspired by you. It builds connection, trust and relatability.

6. Public speaking is such a beautiful way to help the world and grow your

business at the same time. If you are shy, nervous, or think you're a terrible speaker, let's change that and empower you to be amazing on stage.

7. Always be growing. Get Coached. Have a board of directors/mastermind group.

8. Make meetings with you interesting, enjoyable and valuable. Have a wow factor. Know your closing ratio and get coached on how to improve it.

9. Do your annual planning (take my class called "Designing Your Best Year Ever") and be intentional with how you run your business.

10. Give more than you take. Care about people and let it show how much you care about them. Go above and beyond and check in with each client to see how much of their intended outcomes were achieved with you. Sell from a place of true love and caring for your clients

11. Self worth comes before net worth, and you need to know your worth in order to love sales. Plus, this mantra has helped me remember why it's wrong for me to give my services away for free: "When I SPARE YOU the COST of my services, I COST YOU your transformation". People pay more attention when they have purchased the advice.

Helping you LIVE, LOVE and SUCCEED, happily ever after.

Hailey xo

30 Day Challenge

YOUR BEST 30 DAYS

DESIGNING THE LIFE YOU'LL LOVE...
FOR HAPPINESS, WELLBEING, BALANCE AND SUCCESS.

WEEK ONE – YOUR LIFE UPGRADE PREPARATION WEEK

- Happiness intake - take inventory and score yourself out of 10 for each of the categories listed here. 10 is amazing and fulfilled, 0 is empty and not working at all.

- Sleep / Energy / Vibration / Mental Health / Health and Body / Finances / Career / Family / Friends / Home Life / Your Home Itself / Your Love Life / Life Purpose & Passion / Fun & Adventure / Personal Growth

- To help with scoring, ask yourself: How happy and fulfilled am I, with this area of my life, in this moment?

- Consider, and write out if you can, what it would take to make each area a 10 out of 10 for you.

- This month choose your key happiness/life projects (3 or so is ideal) to focus on and really give them some TLC.

- For each of those key areas, explore these questions and write out your answers:

  o How is it now? (Here's where you're allowed to vent and complain.)

  o How would you rather it be? (Describe what a 10 would look like, if it were possible and came true.)

o What can be done about it? (Brainstorm as many items as you can.)

o What WILL you DO about it, and who will you BE to support it, in the next 24 hours?

o For example, to improve my heart health, tomorrow I will walk for 60 minutes in nature and I will be committed to my exercise.

☐ Every day for the next 30 days, to honour your 3 happiness projects, choose your way TO BE, and what you will DO as your action item by the end of each day... set your intentions and promises for the coming day. Or if you are a morning person, you can set these promises in the morning, however, setting them the day before gives you more time to plan and schedule accordingly.

New rituals for a life of joy

You deserve something to look forward to every single day. From now on, choose what to look forward to at the end of your day once you've honoured your commitments, and do the same for the end of each week and month.

The most joyful way to schedule your life

You don't have to take it from me, because this is how I live my life, but you may want to try it for yourself:

☐ You – time for your self care goes on the calendar first.

☐ Connection – next, schedule time to honour your heart, relationships and sense of connection.

☐ Joy – make sure you plan for those moments that light you up and lift you up.

☐ Work – plan your schedule and don't let it suck every hour of your life.

☐ White Space – trust me, you need buffer time to have some wiggle room and space to breathe.

☐ The admin of your life – chores and responsibilities go on last and if you don't have enough time... HIRE OUT!

WEEKS 2, 3 AND 4 – CHOOSE WHICH ITEMS FROM THE LIST BELOW YOU ARE READY TO INCORPORATE INTO YOUR LIFE.

These are the very things that I do, as well as my thousands of clients and students who have enhanced their lives dramatically. This is not new, but it may be new to you as something you do consistently. I believe in you. Choose as many or as few as you feel ready for. You've got this, and I am here to support you.

Nourish

☐ Plan your healthy meals for the day or make sure you are prepped for the plan you already made in advance, which includes what to eat, where and when.

☐ Work with a professional health practitioner to see if you need any health boosters for optimal health and vitality.

Hydrate

☐ Plan your water intake for the day. For example, If I weigh 130 pounds I know I need 65 ounces throughout the day, plus extra for working out... a good measure for me would be to consume 25 ounces before breakfast, 25 before lunch, and at least 15 ounces before dinner... stopping about 30 minutes before my meals. This way I can ensure I will get my water in. What's your water plan?

Rest

- Plan restoration breaks into your day for optimal performance AND well-being. This could be a cup of tea and a 5-minute stretch between every block of focus time...it's up to you.

- Plan your sleep and wake cycle, plus the wind-down and ramp-up times that will support you.

- For example, if I want to sleep from 10pm to 6am, I need to be winding down by 8:30 pm, and certain things in my day have to be complete for me to get into my 'wind down' mode.

- Sleep hygiene matters a lot too. For most people, here are some best practices:

  o Dark room

  o Supportive pillow and mattress

  o No screens by your bed or even in your room

  o Minimize EMF outputting devices in your room, and especially within 3 feet of where you sleep

  o If you must keep your phone in the room, put it on airplane mode

  o Try not to drink a lot of water in the evening – unless you like waking up to pee

  o Temperature regulate in the ways that support you – fan, breathable bedding, etc.

  o Breathe good air – depending on your climate that may include a cool mist humidifier, hepa filter, an essential oils diffuser, etc.

Movement and Circulation

- Choose how you will move your body today, and yes, every day

- What supportive movement will you include in the mix, from stretching, yoga, tai chi, physio exercises, walking, etc... choose which modality of movement will support your wellness goals

☐ Get outside – depending on your climate and health, unless advised against it, try to get outside everyday. Nature is my solace. I plan nature into my day everyday.

☐ Cold Showers – boost circulation while rinsing off in the shower for the final 30 seconds to 3 minutes

☐ Be good to your vessel... every other day my bath gets Epsom salts, an extra long soak with a book to read, a big hunk of rose quarts, and my fave essential oils. Pamper your self!

Mindset, Mood, and Outlook

☐ Visualization, Stillness, Silence, Meditation, Prayer... what ever works for you to set your best mindset in motion – start your days with this before you turn on your phone and start checking notifications. And end your days with this as well... your chosen modality for a peaceful close to the day.

☐ My personal regimen before bed is to say my affirmations mantra, visualize the amazing tomorrow that I intend to create, and press play on my fave guided meditation for sleep with my phone far away and on airplane mode.

☐ You can choose to answer this question before bed, or once you wake up: My dream outcome for the day is???

☐ And finally, set your promised plan in motion, either before bed or when you wake up:

o What is my most important action to take for each of my 3 happiness/life projects?

o What are the ways of being I need to step into, to support my success on my happiness/life projects?

The reader/author in you

- ☐ What beneficial content will you read today?

- ☐ What will you write today? A journal entry, gratitude, your daily plan, poetry, a promise, a letter to a loved one, an apology, an item on your bucket list?

Bonus - Productivity Goddess

- ☐ What thing will you get done today that you have been putting off?

- ☐ Can you spend even 10 minutes knocking something off your list, or tackling just 10 minutes of a bigger project, so you feel that whoosh of pride and accomplishment?

I am excited to hear from you at the beginning of your 30-day challenge to see what you are taking on for yourself, and I would be even more excited to hear from you at the end of your 30 days to learn how your life has lifted as a result. Choose well. You are precious, worthy and capable of raising the quality of your life. Don't expect it to be easy. Expect it to be worth it.

Love and Smiles,

Hailey

www.TheLiftedLid.com

Text 416-797-5856 for support

About the Author

Hailey Patry lives in Oakville, Ontario, Canada, with her husband and three sons. She is a hopeful romantic, who lives for love, and loves to give. She's been nicknamed "World's Happiest Woman" and "World's Best Marriage Mentor". After surviving and thriving from a life of trauma such as rape, cancer, depression, abuse, divorce and more... she has true empathy and compassion for your personal situation. Now that she's created her life, to be filled with happiness and love, she wants to share happiness and love with YOU!

Hailey runs a private coaching and counselling practice seeing clients around the world, on Zoom. She makes house calls in the Halton region and the Greater Toronto Area and offers a unique 1-day relationship makeover session, that clients rave about, as the most transformative day in their entire relationship. Hailey also certifies other professionals in her famous I.D.E.A.L. LOVE method, to become Marriage Mentors.

She is best known for her work in 3 main areas, as:

1. Your Marriage Mentor and Relationship Repair Specialist
2. Your True Happiness Coach
3. The Happy Business coach

Through her work as Your True Happiness Coach, Hailey helps you overcome depression, anxiety, trauma and devastating life transitions. She helps you raise your confidence, your self-worth and the quality of your life in all 12 key areas which include: Your Sleep, Energy and Vibration, Health and Body. Your Mental Health and Mindset, Personal Growth, Your Love Life and Sense of Connection/ Support. Your Home Life and Location, your Finances and Your Career or sense of Life Purpose and Passion. Plus your relationships with Friends, Family and the amount of Fun and Adventure in your life.

As a Marriage Mentor with a specialty in infidelity, radical forgiveness, addiction and trauma, Hailey helps you fall in love with your partner again, rewrite your relationship, gain closure from the past and design the relationship of your dreams. She also helps each spouse become the best individual you can be. She lovingly offers unlimited emergency text support between sessions and will help you work on the meaningful areas of your relationship including: Communication, Respect, Love/Kindness, Forgiveness/Peace, Intimacy/Romance, Communication, Trust, Appreciation, Division-of-labour, Fun/Adventure, Finances and Parenting/ Family Values.

Hailey is a professional speaker, corporate facilitator and 3 x #1 International bestselling author. She is the award-winning author of HAPPY LOVE – 5 Essential Steps to Help Frustrated Couples Fall in Love Again. As the founder of www.The Lifted Lid.com she helps GOOD people, actually live a GOOD life...so you can make life happen FOR you, instead of it happening TO you.

If you, your marriage, or your organization can benefit from a LIFT, it would be her pleasure to gift you a complimentary coaching session. Please text Hailey to book at (416)797-5856.

When she is not on-stage touching audiences or in session with her private clients, you'll find Hailey hiking with her family, kayaking, cooking up healthy alkaline meals, cuddling with her kids or out with her husband, on their weekly date night.

Contact Information
Hailey Patry, Master Coach in Radical Forgiveness
Company: The Lifted Lid
Email: Hailey@TheLiftedLid.com
LinkedIn: www.linkedin.com/in/hailey-patry-theliftedlid/
Facebook: www.facebook.com/TheLiftedLid.com
Website: www.TheLiftedLid.com

Dedication

I dedicate this book to my husband, my two sons, my family members for whom I was able to provide loving care, and to all the clients I have been blessed to serve.

Tammy Spitzer

Movement Enhances Life
EXPLORING PHYSICAL AND EMOTIONAL PILLARS
OF WELLNESS THROUGH THE SENSES

Have you struggled with pain? Do you find that you move more slowly, more stiffly? Are you unable to get up and down from the floor to play with your kids or grandkids? Do you struggle with emotional or mental fatigue that has kept you in a fog much of the time? Do you lack joy?

Would you like to learn a method to help you lessen or eliminate your pain both physically and emotionally? Would you like to learn how to move with freedom and ease? Would you like to learn how to quickly spiral down to the floor or spiral up from the floor to play with your kids or grandkids joyfully? You can learn how to lower yourself in a spiraling down motion that eases the effort to get to the floor. This lesson was my dad's favorite exercise, and I taught him to do it when he was 82, and he did it successfully and joyfully. Would you like to learn some movement lessons and natural solutions to help you out of that fog? And to not only enjoy life more comprehensively but also have more fun and joy doing it?

My life experiences, career, and unique skill sets give me the ability and wisdom to quickly and sustainably give you solutions to these pain points. I've been a Physical Therapist for over three decades, working mainly with the senior population in various settings, especially in long-term care facilities. I am also an Essential Oils Expert and Educator, emphasizing the powerful way oils can elevate, even transcend, our emotions and mood while improving our overall health. I have also been a caregiver for some of my dearest family members five times during this decade. I felt honored and grateful to have this precious time with each of them.

In my early years as a Physical Therapist, my emphasis was on helping people relieve their pain and stiffness, restore functional movement, help a person who could not walk or use their arms or legs after a devastating stroke or brain injury. We would review therapy goals and their personal goals together. Then I would determine the best plan to achieve those goals and then teach them how to continue this independently to return to their home.

MY HOLISTIC JOURNEY EMERGED

"What I'm after isn't flexible bodies, but flexible brains...Actually, what I'm after is to restore people to their human dignity"- Moshe Feldenkrais.

My philosophy of wellness changed when I began to study the Feldenkrais Method ® in 2000. I not only looked at the body physically but emotionally, spiritually, and mentally through a new holistic lens. I had 160 hours of training in this method over four years. I spent countless hours experiencing many of the same lessons I now teach. Even from the beginning of my training, I felt a calmness. I had experienced depression and anxiety much of my life, so I knew that I had made a personal transformation. I was experiencing difficulty sleeping before that, and I recall that I profoundly and peacefully slept well after my first experience. I remember falling asleep briefly during my first lesson, and even though I wondered if I had missed the content, it felt delicious. My husband noticed a calming effect in me and often saw a similar calmness, after these lessons, in the clients that came to our wellness center.

Most of my clients that have used this method have had positive and often significant results. Two of these were so transformative that they left an impression on me for years. I utilized this method with a man unable to move his arm because of a stroke thirteen years earlier. After an hour, he was able to bring his hand to his mouth. His wife was with him, and she teared up, saying, "I've not seen him do that since he had his stroke."

I also worked with a woman that came to see me for only one visit at my wellness center. In her intake, she stated she was struggling emotionally and felt stressed. I gave her a Functional Integration ® session, which takes the client through reasonably passive movements, helping her whole body integrate like a fine concerto, to achieve these results. Something shifted on an emotional level for her during that session, and she left there feeling she would be "OK and knowing she could handle her circumstances." I could see ease in her whole demeanor. I made sure she was safe and encouraged her to receive the therapeutic follow-up she needed, but it showed me that making a change somewhere in the body can change other aspects of oneself, even profoundly. Feldenkrais is an educational process that helps people use their nervous system to organize their body movements and affect emotional wellbeing.

The Feldenkrais Method ® can help a person rekindle their natural abilities based on a self-discovery process using subtle movement and awareness. Moshe Feldenkrais, (rhymes with rice) founder of this method, was a renowned engineer and physicist. He was also an athlete, achieving a black belt in Judo. He sustained an injury to his knee, and physicians told him it would require surgery to return to an athletic level. He refused to take their recommendations and began to study everything he could to heal himself, including how babies progressed from rolling to crawling to walking during their developmental stages, which was instrumental in forming his method. *https://feldenkrais.com/feldenkrais-method-faqs/*

LESS IS MORE!

Learning to move with less effort makes daily living easier. You can use this premise to become more comfortable while working at your computer, occasionally taking brief "awareness breaks" by adjusting your posture and where your eyes focus. Performance in a favorite hobby or sport can improve by reducing unnecessary muscle tension or exertion. Getting down to the floor to play with your children and grandchildren can become simple, fun, and painless. There are also other beautiful lessons, like getting up from a bed more efficiently, lessening pain in the back and neck. Many people use a rocking motion through their abdominals when getting out of bed, that puts a lot of pressure on their neck muscles. Next time you get out of bed, try rolling toward your front, allowing the head to passively come up last to reduce the neck's effort and often rids neck pain.

These gentle lessons can make many life tasks simpler. With this method, "LESS IS MORE." Feldenkrais ® focuses on the relationship between movement, thinking, feeling, and sensing. This style reflects "brain-muscle learning," a neuromuscular re-education process. It has many applications, including addressing pain, improving function or high performance, working with developmental difficulties or neurological problems, and healthy aging.

Feldenkrais lessons are offered in two ways, enabling you to discover which learning style works best for you or a combination of both. Awareness Through Movement ® lessons are verbally led and taught to groups or individuals, live or virtually, or studied alone from recordings, transcripts, or memory. Many lessons are only twenty to forty-five minutes. Even if you have just short bursts of time to devote to this, you can make profound changes with awareness. During Functional Integration ® sessions, which generally last thirty to sixty minutes, the practitioner works with the client one-on-one by communicating through touch, words, and movement. The teacher guides the student toward self-discovery. Regardless of which learning style you choose or a combination of both, the Feldenkrais Method can help anyone overcome limits caused by limited movement, stress, or health issues. https://feldenkrais.com/feldenkrais-method-faqs/

I offer an innovative way to move out of pain and into the freedom of movement that allows the brain to process the easiest and most unique ways to move more efficiently with less effort. This process helps you tap into the wisdom of your nervous system, allowing your brain to create new pathways and improve function. "Neuroplasticity" is the rewiring of neural pathways, which is exciting because we now know this continues throughout life, even in our older years. Moshe understood neuroplasticity way before it became well understood by the scientific community. As you learn new and better ways to move, breathing can become easier, balance and coordination may improve, pain and discomfort can lessen, sleep can become more restorative, and resilience and mental clarity can improve.

WHAT FELDENKRAIS ® IS NOT

Feldenkrais is not an exercise program, a chiropractic adjustment, or a massage. Feldenkrais is not an exercise as in traditional physical therapy. It uses gentle movements within a manageable range, avoiding overstretching. You do not need to sustain positions as required as in yoga. You are not required to be flexible. Yogis may find this method helps achieve difficult or uncomfortable postures. It differs from tai chi in that new learning is always encouraged to continue, versus perfecting one long series of specific movements. There is no need to master skills or a high level of physical conditioning like many martial arts. Feldenkrais can become a daily mindful movement practice as a beautiful way for self-care. You can use it as a moving meditation, and you can even use it to improve your everyday movements, even to the mundane like brushing your teeth, or to the more complex of improving your sports performance and hobbies. Nearly every-one can benefit from the Feldenkrais Method. https://feldenkrais.com/feldenk-rais-method-faqs/

OTHER HEALING MODALITIES

Pain and stiffness can also be addressed by many other complementary modal-ities as well. Reiki is a beautiful modality that uses universal energy that helps individuals release their innate healing. It is calming and soothing to the body, mind, and soul. Acupuncture or acupressure, chiropractic care, massage therapy, chi gong, just to name a few, can be valuable in easing pain.

"Movement is Life."-Moshe Feldenkrais.

I want to explore the topic of movement with you. Through my experience, I've seen how people who live sedentary lives, whether by choice or by physical limitations or pain, limit their movement throughout the day, often creating a cycle of less movement. According to an NHIS study in 2019, about 20.4% of adults experience chronic pain in their lifetime. People often seek complementary or alternative practices when traditional medicine has not eliminated their pain as a last-ditch effort.

In physics, Newton's First Law of Motion explains inertia. Let us apply it to personal activity. "A body at rest tends to stay at rest, and a body in motion tends to stay in motion unless acted on by an external force." It usually takes more effort to initiate a movement than to carry it out. Once you stop something, like an exercise program, it is often difficult to start it back up. Some of you may have physical challenges. Some of you may be in excellent physical shape and just want to tweak your performance. Start wherever you are in your physical health and set an intention to make daily actionable improvements. Use inertia to your advantage, "a body in motion tends to stay in motion" by taking even a tiny step. If you are just starting a walking program, and have physical challenges, maybe you have to walk to the next room and back. Just start walking for five minutes if you aren't active. Begin with a few deep breaths and build up to ten. Park farther away from the store or take stairs versus an elevator. Small changes add up. Then it gets easier to keep moving forward. Starting is nearly halfway there.

Make physical movement a daily priority. Build up to one hour of movement daily, broken into a few bouts over the day if you need. I challenge you to develop 20 ways to increase your daily activity to give yourself plenty of options. What is your favorite way to move? Maybe you are like me, and you love to dance. If you are a walker or runner, where do you go? Perhaps you love to walk on your hands. My brother was known for walking on his hands down the hallways in our school. Maybe you love yoga, tai chi, chi gong. Perhaps you find joy in getting down on the floor while playing with your kids or grandkids. Maybe you like to go bowling, skating, snorkeling or swimming? How long has it been since you rolled down a hill just for the fun of it or swung on swings? Or climbed across the monkey bars? Maybe your thing is an amusement park. Perhaps you are a person that uses a pedometer, and your goal is to increase the number of steps you take over time. Many set a goal of 10,000 steps. Now go and do what works for you.

Newton's Third Law of Motion is essentially "For every action, there is an equal and opposite reaction." In Gay Hendricks's book, "The Big Leap," Gay states, "resistance is hard." If exercise is strenuous for you, then reframe it as a challenge. Know that the resistance you feel is because the task is more extensive than you desire or have experienced. Look at the "pushback as progress." There will be a "new resistance" at each "new level." The moment you start to feel resistance, know that you are making enough progress that the opposing forces feel the need to hold you back. Never give up. Just keep going. (The Big Leap, Gay Hendricks,2010, HarperCollins Publishing.)

Here is a simple but powerful technique from Mel Robbins, a motivational speaker and author of The 5 Second Rule. Mel states, "The moment you have an instinct to act on a goal, you must physically move within 5 seconds, or your brain will stop you. 5-4-3-2-1-GO!" Look at the small changes you can make over time, and these can become life-changing moments. Maybe you just need a slight nudge when your internal drive is low, then use The 5 Second Rule and see what happens."

A study, Metacognition | Center for Teaching | Vanderbilt University, from Vanderbilt University Center for Teaching, in 2013, explains the term metacognition.

The 5 Second Rule is a simple technique that is an excellent example of metacognition useful in helping trick the brain into achieving its goals. By feeling out of control of your life circumstances, it affects functioning in the prefrontal cortex, responsible for important things like planning, decision making, and working toward goals. From Mel Robbins, "When you count down 5-4-3-2-1-GO, you're taking deliberate action. The countdown pushes you out of autopilot. And when you act, you're exercising control, and you're turning on your prefrontal cortex." Another simple technique from Mel Robbins is every time you pass a mirror, smile and give yourself a high five. It brings you joy and makes it easier to keep going. (Key reference: The Five Elements of the 5-Second Rule, Mel Robbins. April 25, 2018 Blog.) In Susan Jeffers book title, she says, "Feel The Fear, and Do It Anyway ®."

There you have it, if you go for a walk or run in the morning, then have your sneakers under your bed. When you are ready to get up- just say 5-4-3-2-1 GO. Use this anytime you need the impetus to start an activity, exercise, or any task you are resisting and see what happens.

EASY NATURAL SOLUTIONS

Here are some natural solutions that I like to use to improve daily health habits. You can make a fruit and veggie wash, using one-half cup of water and apple cider vinegar each and five drops of lemon and orange essential oil each to a spritzer bottle. Improve focus by opening a bottle of lemon essential oil and take two beautiful breaths to clear brain fog. Just add twenty drops of lemon essential oil to one-half cup of white vinegar in a glass spray bottle. Use this to spritz on clothing stains and then wash for an effective stain remover. Mix a half cup of baking soda and ten drops of tea tree essential oil to one-quarter cup of white vinegar and let sit in the toilet for 15 mins to disinfect a toilet. Visit *www. FindingJoyInCaregiving.com* and request a free guide for healthy cleaning for more recipes to replace the many chemicals in everyday cleaning products to reduce "your overall toxic load."

I also offer new caregivers of parents the necessary and innovative strategies and techniques they need to provide exceptional care delivered in a joyful way for both them and their loved ones. I am building a community of caregivers and their loved ones:

- Share positive moments of caregiving experiences with like-minded people.
- Discover easier and less painful ways to move, through Feldenkrais ® lessons.
- Learn how to experience essential oils to improve mood, find joy, and clean up your environment.
- Learn how to start your day with a positive mindset to manage everyday stresses
- Discover strategies and processes to simplify your day and more.

SELF-CARE

Have you ever struggled with self-care? How about being too tired to change your clothes or take your make-up off before bed?   Do you feel like you are giving all your time and energy away by caring for others? Then you lack the energy or desire for even the most minor but essential things for yourself, like brushing your teeth or even showering? Or remembering your medications? Are you an empath, a super mom or caregiver, a healthcare worker or a teacher? Have you ever sabotaged your self-care just because you're too tired?

I suffered from depression and anxiety for nearly half of my life. I had medications for these, but they rarely ever helped me feel joy, just OK and sometimes; NOT. I still take medicine, but I did find a solution that gave me a way to feel more joy. *Remember that not everyone will have the same results, and there are no guarantees; I am sharing my personal experience with you. I learned about essential oils when we had our wellness center, but I hadn't made it a regular practice to use them personally. In 2013, a friend introduced me to essential oils through a company that focuses highly on finding the highest and purest quality of essential oils. They have a team of scientists, researchers, and chemists and provide vital education backed by scientific evidence. For a few weeks, I had begun using citrus oils in a diffuser. My husband pointed out that I seemed happier recently. The citrus oils had a positive impact on my mood. He was right, something changed, and for me, it was the use of these high-quality pure and potent oils.

WHAT ARE ESSENTIAL OILS?

Essential oils are volatile compounds found in various parts of the plant, including the fruit, seed, resin, bark, peel. They give the plant its scent and protect the plant from external threats.

(Modern Essentials. A Contemporary Guide to the Therapeutic Use of Essential Oils. 5th Edition. Aroma Tools. 1351 W. 800 N. Orem, UT 84057.)

When tiny molecules enter our bodies, they can protect us from many internal and external threats. Essential oils are not new. They are well-researched, safe when appropriately used, and are effective with proper education.

I will focus on the aromatic use of essential oils, which is the most popular and most straightforward.

According to www.pubmed.gov, diffusing oils can be powerful. We used to think that our brain could detect about 10,000 different scents/ smells- like an essential oil. Although according to BrainFacts.org, it is vastly more than that. Our sense of smell is the most rudimentary of our senses. As we open a bottle of essential oil, like Rose, the scent enters through our nose, which is part of the olfactory system, and then it is processed by the portion of the brain that is responsible for controlling our sense of smell. From there, aromatic pathways connect the scent to the part of our brain where memories and experiences are stored. As the aroma travels through aromatic pathways, memories can be triggered, giving us an emotional response.

When it comes to aromatherapy, essential oils are generally considered uplifting or calming. Floral oils are often calming due to their chemical makeup. Most oils from the spice, citrus, or mint families are uplifting because they produce a refreshing and energizing aroma. No two people will have the same response to an essential oil but choosing calming or energizing oils, based on which one you need emotionally is a good start. Our reactions to smells relate to past experiences, preferences, genetic makeup, and the environment.

(Modern Essentials. A Contemporary Guide to the Therapeutic Use of Essential Oils. 5th Edition. Aroma Tools. 1351 W. 800 N. Orem, UT 84057.)

MY PERSONAL FAVES!

I want to share some of my favorite essential oils with you. Frankincense, often considered the king of oils, supports healthy cellular function, supports immune/nervous and digestive systems, soothes skin appearance, promotes relaxation, and more. Lavender soothes occasional mild skin irritations, helps promote restful sleep, lessens anxious feelings, and more. Among other benefits, lemon can cleanse and purify the air and clean surfaces like countertops, support healthy respiratory and digestive systems, and uplifts mood. A few drops of Rosemary in a diffuser may help concentration, may aid memory, and lessen occasional mental fatigue. Peppermint can be a natural bug repellant, and it can cool and energize the body. In my opinion, there are many products now being advertised with essential oils in them, so more precautions are needed. Visit: www.doterra.com/tammyspitzer for more info.

Since this is only a brief overview of essential oils, I recommend that if you are unfamiliar with oils, educate yourself and then become your own best advocate for yourself and your family. I like Dr. Eric Zielinski, D.C. 's book, The Healing Power of Essential Oils, as a good primer for safe practices with essential oils. Tips on Safety

Whether you are new to essential oils or have been using them for years, this practice can be valuable as one part of an overall wellness plan. Essential oils can be helpful for cleaning, cooking, maintaining good health, and promoting wellbeing. Here are some safety measures to consider.

- ☐ Start slow, learn safety precautions.
- ☐ Be responsible- they are potent, so a little is usually all that is needed.
- ☐ It is always a safe practice to dilute oils for skin. Citrus oils are generally photosensitive, so do not use them on exposed skin that will be in the sun for up to twelve hours or when in a sunbed.
- ☐ I do not feel they are a magic pill or bullet but used appropriately and safely; they can assist your body in helping it to regain or maintain its homeostasis.

(The Healing Power of Essential Oils. Eric Zielinski, D.C. 2018. Dreamscape Media, LLC. Publisher.)

Remember that physical wellness is multi-faceted, and we all carry our definition of what physical wellness means. In addition to movement, remember that your overall energy and stamina, good quality sleep, proper hydration and nutrition, overall strength and flexibility, emotional wellbeing, and a clean and peaceful environment are essential components.

HOW CAN I HELP?

If you would like to know more about The Feldenkrais Method®, using Essential

Oils for general wellness and mood management, and discussing essential strategies on creating a mindset of joy, it would be my honor to take that journey with you. I have witnessed how these and other strategies have made differences in how people move out of pain and stiffness and feel they honor their bodies through using essential oils, mindset, and other holistic practices. You may book a complimentary strategy call with me on my websites to see if we are a good fit.

The information provided in this chapter is designed to provide helpful information on the various subjects discussed. This chapter is not intended as a substitute for medical advice from a physician, physical therapist, or other healthcare practitioners. It is not intended to diagnose, treat, cure or prevent. The reader should feel free to contact their physician or healthcare practitioner. The reader assumes full responsibility for their own choices, actions, and results.

"Rekindle that curiosity, wonder, and joy that you had as a child. Embrace it and allow it to bring out the best version of you."

Tammy Spitzer

30 Day Challenge

Goals: Move with more ease, manage your emotions better, clean up your environment.

Benefits of this challenge:

- New or upgraded wellness plan with emphasis on increased movement.
- Begin to look for simpler and more efficient ways to move during your everyday routines.
- Healthier, happier you

LET US EXPLORE:

1. To know where you are going, you must know where you are NOW to narrow the gap. On Day 1, Measure the 8 areas below on a scale of 1 to 10. Repeat this at End of Month to measure your progress. Ten is "Wow, I'm nailing this area, " and One is "I need a lot of help in this area." For example, for "Energy/Stamina," you may rate yourself today at a 6/10 or 60% of where you want to be. Now, grab your journal and write what it would take to reach the next level in each area by month end. For example, if you start an area at 6, what would it take to get to level 7 by the end of the month?

Areas to measure	Day 1	End of Month
1. Energy/ Stamina	_____	_____
2. Ease of Movement-Lack of pain/stiffness	_____	_____
3. Sleep-fall asleep easily, wake up refreshed	_____	_____

4. Hygiene-Do you struggle to make the time?   _____   _____

5. Hydration and Good Nutrition   _____   _____

6. Strength/Flexibility   _____   _____

7. Emotional Well-being   _____   _____

8. Environment   _____   _____

2. Get your journal or go to the side notes of this month's challenge; list 20 ways you may enjoy increasing your daily movement routine. Write for at least two minutes. Select at least five of these, pencil them on your calendar. Schedule a few that can rekindle that child in you. Plan it out, and maybe you need to make specific arrangements. Block the time you need. Be adventurous and playful.

3. Do a body scan (see the following page) in bed each morning, recheck it before bedtime if able- and get the scan down to one or two minutes.

4. Explore the Five Second Rule to take quicker action toward getting out of bed and during your movement routines. Keep your sneakers near the bed if you start your day with a walk or run.

5. Give yourself a high-five every time you look in a mirror to shift toward inner JOY.

6. Pick something simple you do, like brushing your teeth. I noticed that I was making a fist in my supporting arm at the sink, which caused unnecessary tension in my body. When I opened my hand, I felt a release of tension in my arm and even through my whole body. See if you could simplify that task, or another daily task, like getting up from your bed in the morning. Make it feel even more effortless. Remember, LESS IS MORE. Sense if you are holding unnecessary tension anywhere, then just release it.

7. Increase your movement every day- by time, frequency or variety. Write your

personal goals in your journal. "I will increase my activity/movement to _____ minutes per day, or I will raise my steps per day from _____ to _____.

8. Improve your environment. Make at least 1 DIY cleaner using natural ingredients, including pure essential oils for your home or car, or a hand sanitizer. Use a diffuser to help clean the air. To access a free download for Everyday Ways/ Recipes That You Can Enjoy for a Natural Lifestyle, Visit: www.FindingJoyInCaregiving.com

9. Add a diffuser and an uplifting or calming essential oil to your kitchen, bathroom, bedroom, and main living area to enhance your positive emotions.

10. Keep in mind that your physical wellness is more than just movement. It is also about restorative sleep, good hydration, proper nutrition, cleaning up your environment, minimizing stress, and good emotional health. Journal your thoughts on improving this and make at least a slight improvement in each area.

"Make the impossible possible, the possible easy, the easy elegant."

Moshe Feldenkrais

TRY THIS BODY SCAN INFLUENCED BY TEACHINGS OF MOSHE FELDENKRAIS

What would it mean to you if you could lie on your back without discomfort? Then move to stand and walk with ease. Then easily reach above your head or spiral to the floor with ease. Start here.

Begin by lying on your back. If you can lay your legs out long, do so. You can roll a towel under your knees if needed.

Honor wherever you start. Notice how that feels in your body. Are you comfortable? Are you in pain? Restless? I will ask you many questions. Just reflect on the answers, do not change your position.

How are your legs positioned? Are your feet rolled out or rolled in? One in and one out? Or pointed toward the ceiling? How much space is under your knees?

Now focus on your breath. Do you notice if it's shallow or deep? Fast or slow? Is your chest expanding and contracting? Is your abdomen lifting and lowering? Maybe your shoulders lift and fall as you breathe. Don't change anything. Just be aware.

Now how is your back contacting the floor? How is your head lying? Is it straight or tilted to the side? How much space is between your neck and the floor? Could your hand or fist slip easily under this space?

How does your spine contact the floor? Can you sense how part of your spine is resting comfortably and easily on the floor where other parts of your spine do not touch the floor at all? Let that sink in. Maybe now you are aware of a gentle curve in your spine, where there is some space under the neck and low back, but the middle of the back is fully supported. Maybe the low back is now supported fully by the floor. Notice if your breath feels different now. REST and BE.

This time, be aware of how you have positioned your arms. Are they both resting by your side or on your chest or abdomen? How are your hands placed, palms down, palms up, or halfway in between? How far are your arms from your sides? How far are your shoulders from the floor- several inches or close to the floor? Can you feel where your shoulder blades are? Rest again.

Check in with your overall body. Maybe something has changed. Maybe more of your body is now resting comfortably on the floor. Now slowly get up from this position, move to sitting, standing, and then walking when ready. Notice how your body feels and advances in each of these positions. Maybe you can apply some of this thinking to other movements?

I recommend that you take a few minutes to do this at the beginning and end of your day. You may feel this awareness spreading to many of your daily tasks. Feldenkrais® lessons focus on teaching the nervous system how to learn, designed for the whole body, mind, and spirit.

Receive a free audio recording of this body scan to use while doing your body scan. Visit: www.findingJoyInCaregiving.

About the Author

Tammy Spitzer, PT, GCFP (Guild-Certified Feldenkrais Practitioner), is a Physical Therapist, Caregiver Specialist, Holistic Practitioner, Movement Educator, Mentor Expert, and an Essential Oils Expert and Educator. She has been a physical therapist for over 30 years, serving many of those years working with seniors in her tri-state area. Tammy has worked in various settings, including skilled nursing facilities, including dementia units. Her other accolades include serving as a Neurology Professor for a physical therapy program, starting up two physical therapy departments/programs, and serving several years as a rehab/physical therapy department supervisor.

As a Physical Therapist, Tammy was initially intrigued by the physical pillar of wellness, but her desire to help people holistically dramatically shifted around 2000. Tammy then focused more intensely on holistic and complementary approaches that considered the emotional, spiritual, and mental aspects. She underwent a four-year intensive training program to become a Movement Educator as a Feldenkrais Practitioner ®. Tammy is a Reiki Master, and she specializes in the use of essential oils for overall wellness. Tammy and her husband operated their wellness center from 2005-2009, collaborating with other healthcare practitioners. At their wellness center, Tammy worked with an aromatherapist and began to understand how essential oils were beneficial for many health issues, especially in women's health and overall emotional wellbeing. She has a passion for sharing how essential oils can help support the body emotionally, physically, and spiritually. Tammy has taught essential oil classes in a variety of settings. She also enjoys getting the opportunity to work with families in their homes.

Tammy has had the unique opportunity to be a caregiver for five of her loved ones in this decade. She considers this to be a gift and an honor. She desires to inspire, educate and uplift other caregivers to find joy in their caregiving experiences.

She is a proud partner in Powerful Women Today, where she is a Mentor Expert.

Tammy considers herself a lifelong learner. She continues to improve her physical therapy and holistic practices through extensive continuing education. Her passion for personal development has led her to study with several personal development coaches. God and family are both central to her. She loves creating magical moments for her family and the teams she has worked with, inspiring them to open up to life's possibilities.

Contact information

Tammy Spitzer, PT

Company: Finding Joy in Caregiving

Email: t.spitzer01@gmail.com

LinkedIn: www.linkedin.com/in/tammy-spitzer-b3a687199

Facebook: www.facebook.com/OilsWork

Website: www.findingjoyincaregiving.com

Dedication

For my Mom and Dad who shaped me into the woman I am,

The loves of my life, Austin and Brooke,

And my beloved Craig

Karen Porter

I'll never forget the day in June 2015. It was 2 days before my daughter's high school graduation. I was in the psychiatric ward of our local hospital. It had happened again. I was alone, cold a nd confined by these four walls, but even worse, I was confined in my brain. I wanted to escape, but I couldn't. Even if I could leave this room, leave this hospital, I could never get away from my brain...

Oh my god, the shame of being here. I was beyond any tears. I was empty inside. How did my brain and my body do this to me once again? I'd been hospitalized three times previously in the same condition – wanting to get out of this life. And it's hard to understand, it's even foreign to me now.

When I realized I was still alive, after what I'd done, I felt so much remorse. When my husband came into the room, all I could do was repeat, "I'm so sorry", the same thing that I'd written on the note. I didn't know how my brain could be so screwed up, but it was. I don't know what point it was – that day or the next, when I realized that my daughter's graduation was imminent. I felt so sick for my kids. They were busy with their own adolescent lives, but I felt like such a failure. A failure when I could no longer do my job, when I didn't feel like I was caring for my children like I should, when I couldn't love my husband like I should. When I'd let everyone down, my family and myself.

And never did this go outside of our immediate family of four. My sister, sister-in-law and Mom and Dad knew that I was experiencing depression, but they never knew how bad it was. That is something that my husband and I always kept to ourselves... because of society's stigma, the stigma that even we felt about mental illness. Even a nurse at the hospital said, "How could you do such a thing? You have children."

The doctor monitored me for two days, and finally on the day of her graduation, after much begging by my husband and myself, he finally agreed to let me leave the hospital for that afternoon, released with my husband to attend my daughter Brooke's graduation. I got ready with the help of my sister-in-law, who we'd finally told what was going on. I was the one who called her before the hospital nurses realized I had my cell phone and took it away. Apparently you're not to have a cell phone in the psychiatric ward. I actually felt a little better for my husband that my sister-in-law knew, because at least he wasn't carrying the burden of "me" by himself. I don't remember much about my daughter's graduation, although both of her grandparents were there also. I know that I didn't look good. We told them that I was in the hospital because of my stomach. It was not so far fetched with all of my IBS issues.

It might be a good time to backtrack a little and explain. I had a life that most people would dream of. I had a wonderful husband, beautiful children, cars, house, cottage. But for almost 30 years I had dealt with severe IBS (Irritable Bowel Syndrome) and debilitating bouts of depression and anxiety. There's a saying that everything starts in the gut, and it's so true. Pain and bloating were a daily occurrence for me, and I would go through bouts with my digestion that would swing from one extreme to the other. I was once hospitalized with a bowel obstruction. I remember the doctor saying, "We'll have to do tests, but we can't rule out cancer." Tests were done, and it was not cancer, but nothing was conclusive. I could only assume the period of constipation before was just more than my body could handle. Then there were the other periods of time when I couldn't get to a washroom fast enough. There were so many times when my daughter would be late for school. She went to a Montessori school and I drove her almost half an hour to get there. So many times I couldn't even make it to school. I'd have to pull into a Tim Horton's, Subway or anyplace that had a bathroom.

But the times that I experienced anxiety and depression were far worse than any digestive issue, bloating or bowel pain. I had a bout with severe and debilitating depression once in my 20's, once in my 30's and twice in my 40's. It would always start with me worrying about things that I didn't normally worry about. The first time it hit, in my 20's, I was working a very stressful management banking position. Things were changing. I don't think I was doing what I thought was expected of me. I don't really know how it got triggered other than that. But that constant stress at work started trickling into everything. I started to be worried about not just work, but everything. My body was tight and anxious all the time. Then it started to affect my sleep. I was too wired to sleep and weeks would go by with me being up half the night, and then awake at 4:30 or 5pm. It started to affect my brain and I couldn't function properly. The little bit of food that I felt like eating (because I was so anxious) just went right through me because of my IBS. That meant that there were very few nutrients going to my brain. It makes sense when I look back at it now. I remember walking into a crisis centre at the hospital a few times. On the third time, they finally admitted me. Being there was awful, but when I was released, I attended an outpatient course and psychiatric meetings where I learned CBT – Cognitive Behavioural Therapy. Eventually, I started to feel better.

I had hoped that after I had children around 30, that I would be more well-rounded and busy with them. I was hoping to be immune from it. But that wasn't the case. I returned to work and it was going okay for a while. But then that same pattern returned. Now I would beat myself up even more. Hadn't I learned anything from my last experience, from the months of courses and psychiatric counselling? Of course that just added to the guilt, and now I had kids to worry about. I always thought I should be able to handle everything. Other women were juggling everything, weren't they? Things went from bad to worse. I was sliding down the slippery slope to my living hell. This time, wanting desperately to get out. Everyone would be better off without me, right? At least that's what I thought.

This would be a good time to mention that I grew up in a wonderful home, but there definitely were perfectionistic tendencies for me to take on. My dad worked tirelessly on his business, building it up to be very successful. My mom was at home, and I didn't realize it until much later in life, but my mom always had things looking perfectly – herself, the house. She would not set foot outside the door unless her hair and make-up were done and she was beautifully dressed. When my mom woke up in the morning, my dad would jokingly say, "Where's the broom you flew in on?" Which to me meant, "You look like a witch". But when she got ready, he was always very complimentary. When I moved into my teens, he'd say the same thing to me. I knew he was joking, but it set something in me that said, you're not good enough until you're all done up. I was the weird kid in high school who wore dress pants and high heels while the other kids were wearing jeans.

My "style" worked out perfectly when I started in the Management Training Program at a bank right out of university. I definitely fit the part – professional and polished looking, strong work ethic, high standards. I think I was the best version of both of my parents in those days. But when I started to slide, it became the perfect storm – I was an unstable, driven, high achieving perfectionist. And my brain had become too familiar with the pattern. Down I went.

Each depressive episode, after a week or more in the hospital and months of outpatient care, I slowly started to improve. And I would never look back because of the stigma. I always tried to look forward and be optimistic. That was my nature. Unfortunately, though I was learning things, it was never enough to keep it away for long. Again, in my early 40's it hit. Each time seemed worse than the last. Each time got longer, and the recovery was slower. But eventually I would feel better.

One day, I attended a healthy cooking class at a grocery store and clicked with the instructor, a nutritionist. I started working with her in hopes of helping my IBS. At the time, I had no idea that it would actually help my brain too. It wasn't until years later that I learned about the gut-brain connection. Even my doctor didn't know about it then. What I found out later was that if something was not great in your digestion, it affected many other areas in your body, especially your brain. Having spent some time with the nutritionist I met, I completely changed my diet. I didn't eat badly before, but I learned what fuelled my body and what didn't, and I felt so much better. Unfortunately, a depressive episode would hit once more. (I knew that I'd come a long way with my nutrition, but there were still things that I needed to learn). I was so interested in the field of nutrition that I'd actually started attending courses. But I was still trying to do my other job (now a mortgage broker rather than a banker), I was trying to start a business, dealing with teenagers, etc. and that same pattern of anxiety, sleep deprivation, weight loss, and digestive issues reared its ugly head again.

This was the last episode, two days before my daughter's graduation. After being released from the hospital, I attended the outpatient hospital programs and psychiatric counselling as I had before. I also sought out psychotherapy, and was finally able to work on the stress piece through mindfulness. For the first six weeks, I was convinced it wasn't helping me, but I persisted. I also tried to do things with friends when I didn't feel like it, and even started volunteering. All of these things combined, in addition to how I was now eating, exercising, and my commitment to myself, helped me return to feeling better. Actually, with my newfound knowledge, I was feeling even better than I'd felt before. I finally felt that I had the tools that I needed to continue to feel good.

I realized that I became very passionate about everything to do with health and wellness of the body and mind. I completed my certification as a Registered Holistic Nutritionist and went on to become certified in Mindfulness in Coaching and Counselling. I finally said to hell with the stigma of my mental health issues. I knew that I had to look back and work with everything that I'd learned in order to completely heal. I didn't want there to be a next time because there was a chance that it could be worse. I was going to do everything in my power to prevent it. I took it one step further and decided to open up about it with others, in a big way. I spoke on stages opening up about my battle with IBS, depression and suicide because I thought that if I could help one other woman, than it would be worth it.

My passion then became my mission and I wanted to do everything in my power to help women to live their best life! Primarily women my age, over 45. My goal was to make the rest of their life, the best of their life! To regain their energy and feel great in their bodies (and minds) so that they could love their life! I wanted women to achieve this easier and in much less time than it took me. The biggest thing was showing them that it was possible. There just needed to be a guide to help break it down.

I know that there is so much information available on the internet and in books. In fact there is too much information, and it's often conflicting. What women need is support and accountability, for tasks to be broken down into manageable chunks, and for reassurance that they're on the right track.

The areas that I focus on to make women feel their best are:

- nutrition
- movement
- stress management
- mindset
- self-fulfillment

NUTRITION

There is no one size fits all. Each one of us is unique, with different DNA and body composition. Working with what is going on with your health and in your life is paramount. I am all about the quality of the food we put into our bodies. I use the analogy of a luxury car. If you saved all of your money and bought a Porsche that required premium gasoline, you would not likely after 4 months decide that you were going to put in a low-grade gasoline. No. You know that peak performance for your car required premium gasoline. And yet, we don't treat our bodies the same way. If you want peak performance for your body and mind, you need premium fuel (ie. good quality food). When I'm choosing what I want to eat, I think about how I want to feel. Making that association with your food can take time, but it makes things so much easier. My two biggest tips when it comes to nutrition are hydration and blood sugar balancing. We need to start drinking water as soon as we wake up, even before coffee or tea. Then thinking about drinking half of your body weight in ounces of water throughout the day. Balancing your blood sugar is important because that's what allows us to feel satiated (satisfied) longer, it gives us consistent energy, it reduces cravings, and it allows our brain to work better. How do we achieve blood sugar balance? It's by having protein, healthy fat and fibre at each meal.

MOVEMENT

It is true that as we age, we need to work on maintaining/building muscle, not just because it looks good, but because it helps our bones, our metabolism, so many things. However, the biggest key to movement is finding something that gives you joy (yes joy!) Exercise should not be a punishment. Sometimes we can even be doing too much, that actually puts stress on the adrenals, but if you do something that you enjoy 5 to 6 times per week for 20 minutes, that is a good start. It could be a brisk walk, getting out in nature, biking, dancing, something that you will enjoy. It's making it a habit that is most important. Then you can work up from there to increase the time and include resistance/light weights.

STRESS MANAGEMENT

This one is big. You could be eating great food and exercising, but if you don't manage stress, not only are you likely to find it difficult to lose weight, your hormones will be out of whack, and you will likely be far from happy. Your body will always be producing higher amounts of cortisol and insulin, and you'll often feel anxious and wired. Things like breathwork, visualization, affirmations, meditation and gratitude are key. These things change the physiology of your brain by creating new neuropathways. This doesn't just affect you while you're doing the activity, but it affects you throughout your day, making you more resilient to whatever you have to tackle in your day. I start everyday with an affirmation. It is, "Good morning. I love you Karen. It's going to be a great day!"

Then I start drinking water. Within the first 5 minutes, I'm outside taking deep breaths and thinking about the 3 things I'm grateful for. My morning routine has a few more things, but that's how it always starts out!

MINDSET

This is another big one. Again, other things can be in place, but if you're not addressing the way you look at things, you will be negatively affected. Our default for the majority of people is negative. Think about when you wake up and look in the mirror. Most women are quick to point out the things that are negative, things that we don't like about ourselves. I always say, imagine if we obsessed about the things we loved about ourselves! I encourage you to make a list – it can be external things like your eyes or your smile, it can be internal things like your empathy or your willingness to learn, it can be things that you've accomplished like university or a recent course or achievement, and finally it can be things that you've overcome. We all have these things. Make that list and refer to it often. There are things that hold us back from where we want to be. They are limiting beliefs that we all have. We picked most of our beliefs up before the age of 8 from our caregivers and those around us. Until it's brought to our attention, we really don't question them. Our limiting beliefs will affect us our whole life if we don't address them.

SELF-FULFILLMENT

Especially as we get older, this becomes increasingly important. Perhaps, now that the kids are older, you have a bit more time for yourself? (Although you may be in a sandwich generation.) Are you doing what you truly enjoy? Are you taking risks and stepping outside of your comfort zone often? Doing what we enjoy and continually expanding and growing are what we were meant to do. That doesn't mean that you have to quit your job. You may find fulfillment in a hobby or outside mission. But really look at all of the areas of your life – relationships, family, occupational, emotional, spiritual, financial, etc.

As I mentioned, this may seem daunting, but with a guide to help you break it down, it is achievable. We all deserve to feel our best, to not only live without disease, but to really thrive. Many women believe, often having been told by their doctors, that what they're experiencing is due to aging or menopause. I believe in giving you the knowledge and support to empower you. You have a say in how you feel. Yes, you can feel and look your best! It just requires that you take action toward your goal and you have guidance while you do it!

30 Day Challenge

FEEL FABULOUS IN 30!

Set at least 15 to 20 minutes aside each day to do this 30 day challenge. Invest in yourself. Think about how you really want to feel in your body today, tomorrow and 15 years from now. Invite a friend. Have an accountability partner! We are going to love ourselves toward our best health!

DAY 1 – LOVING AWARENESS

For the next 5 days think about 1) Forgiving yourself and others. You can write a letter out to yourself or someone else that you truly need to forgive. Forgiveness helps us open up and take action in our best interest. 2) Self-love – pay attention to your self-talk. What do you say when you look at yourself in the mirror in the morning? It's usually negative. But imagine if we obsessed about the things we loved about ourselves?! The first thing I say when I wake up is, "Good morning. I love you Karen. It's going to be a great day." Pay attention to your thoughts, especially the negative ones. We need to get rid of depleting emotions like guilt and shame. Self-care is taking care of your mind and your body, and it's the highest expression of love. 3) Compassion – we each have our own story (and we usually don't know what that story is for others). Have more compassion for yourself (especially as you become aware of your negative thoughts) and for others. 5) Gratitude helps to rewire the brain. Think of 3 things that you're grateful for every morning. When you do this you begin to rewire your brain and you will see more things in your day to be grateful for. The moment you find yourself in anger or sadness, try to think of what you're grateful for.

DAY 5 – AUTONOMIC PAIRING

For the next 5 days, we are going to get more control over our nervous system, in order to regain control over our life and our health. Too often we are in fight or flight mode and cortisol is being released continually. As an example, it is effective when we have to run when being chased by a rabid dog (temporary), not to be long term. So many things in our body are altered when we are stressed (and in fight or flight mode too long). It begins affecting our mood, our metabolism, our weight, and ultimately can lead to disease. We need to get into our parasympathetic nervous system - which is rest and digest. So what can we do? Observe our thoughts. See what triggers us. Take a minimum of 3 deep breaths in the morning, before you eat, and throughout the day whenever you can. Walk out in nature. Slow things down. Stop trying to multi-task. Pair your nervous system with the task at hand.

DAY 15 – NARROWED EATING WINDOW

You don't need to drastically reduce calories, but where your body will benefit (for most people) is to reduce the window of time in which you eat. It's not about starving or going long periods of time without eating. First, stop snacking after dinner. Drink water throughout the day, away from your meals. Try herbal tea if you want a different flavour sometimes. When you eat, make sure to have protein, healthy fat and fibre rich carbohydrates. This will keep you feeling satisfied longer, help to reduce your sugar cravings, help your energy remain consistent and keep your blood sugar balanced. Try to eat breakfast a little later. If you have breakfast at 9am and dinner at 6pm, you are eating in a 9 hour window and not eating in a 15 hour window. You can continue like this or push breakfast out a little later to shorten the window to 8 hours, always listening to your body. Know that your body does adjust. I know this goes against what we used to think about eating breakfast within an hour of waking up. But research has shown it is not necessary. "Breakfast as the most important meal of the day" came about by the cereal industry! Cereal is not a good morning breakfast. It has very little protein (if any) and no healthy fat. Each meal is important – think good quality, nutrient-dense whole food. Limit snacking throughout the day unless you are really hungry.

DAY 20 – REST & RECOVERY

In the Western culture we are so busy "doing" all day and evening that many people don't realize how important rest and recovery is. A good nights sleep actually begins with a good morning routine – sunlight exposure in the morning. It actually affects our circadian rhythm. Our internal clock signals our body. Other things like reduction of overhead light in the evening, no screens 2 hours before bed, keeping bedtime and wake-time consistent, sleeping in darkness, getting to bed between 10 and 11pm and getting 7 to 8 hours are equally important. Sleep deprivation causes us to not only feel tired and have less energy, it increases cravings, causes us to consume more calories, and it also plays a huge role in our brain function (increased negative thoughts, poor decisions, and it can also affect memory). Sleep is important!

DAY 25 – JOYFUL MOVEMENT

Do something you enjoy, something that brings you joy! Try to do 20-30 minutes 5-6 days per week. It should be a celebration of your body, not a punishment for eating. Dance, walk, bike, do yoga. Make it something you look forward to!

About the Author

While outwardly navigating a successful 23 year career in the financial industry, Karen inwardly battled severe IBS, anxiety and debilitating bouts of suicidal depression that left her hospitalized and grasping for her life. Forced to re-evaluate everything and take her health into her own hands, Karen started looking for assistance outside of the medical paradigm and into methods and modalities that treated her body as a whole, rather than just treating symptoms of illness.

Karen's certification as a Registered Holistic Nutritionist and subsequent

Mindfulness Coaching and Counselling training, combined with her own healing experience, allowed her to finally find the much needed answers to gain control of her physical and mental health, and learn the tools required to feel happy, energetic, focused and radiant!

Her health, and consequently her life, entirely shifted and she felt compelled to help as many women as possible.

Karen is passionate about helping women over 45 to regain their energy and feel great in their bodies, so they can live their best life! As a Women's Health & Wellness Coach she takes the confusion and overwhelm out of nutrition, movement, stress management and mindset, while empowering women to feel happy and fulfilled. Other desirable side effects when working with Karen include weight loss, better sleep, hormone balancing and increased confidence!

Her signature program – *Your Best Life Reset* – offers results that are nothing short of life-changing! She also offers a Free *Feel Fabulous in 5 Day Challenge* and Masterclasses to help you make small changes to get big results.

She also offers wellness retreats at her beautiful lakefront cottage in Haliburton – immersing women in an unforgettable experience for the body, mind and soul, that leaves them empowered and equipped to feel and live their best life!

Karen has been featured on Global TV, Breakfast Television, CP24, and Rogers TV.

Contact Information

Karen Porter, RHN

Company: Karen Porter Your Radient Life

Email: karen@karenporter.ca

LinkedIn: www.linkedin.com/in/karen-porter-548590169

Facebook: www.facebook.com/karen.porter.7330

Website: www.karenporter.ca

Dedication

To my partner, best friend, and love, Michael Toprover.

Leona Krasner

---

30 DAYS TO BETTER RELATIONSHIPS

Relationships are hard. There. I said it. They take a surprising amount of effort to maintain at an ideal level. And the worst part is when resentment starts to creep in. When you begin to cloak yourself in armor during the good times, because you are just waiting for the bad times to bite you. It becomes an anticipation game of just waiting to get let down again. Or - worse - waiting to feel as though you are a priority in this person's life. Or walking on eggshells with every single word that comes out of your mouth, for fear of setting them off in some way.

I've been there. With friends, family, boyfriends, even my husband. My husband and I used to play the silent treatment game early on in our relationship, any time one of us got upset with the other. Then came some attacks and insults and past grievances, and only then would we talk about what we needed to do better. Along the way, I dove into a rather ridiculous number of personal development books, launched a matrimonial law firm, and got to assist folks in navigating some truly egregious relationships. This challenge represents a culmination of those techniques and strategies that have worked best for my clients, friends, family, and myself, both personally and professionally.

So, why do a 30-day relationship challenge, anyway? To repair the relationships you really want to salvage that you can already see sinking. To strengthen and weather-proof those already-strong relationships you currently have. And to let those relationships that are hurting you go.

By embarking on this 30-day challenge, your stress levels will go down, you will feel a deeper connection with your people, and you will begin to grow the roots of your relationship habits for years to come. It's going to be hard. People are going to tell you things you're going to have to fix too. You will have to be open to being vulnerable for this to work. Good news, though: people don't like ice cubes, at least when those ice cubes are people. Further, contrary to what my mother always told me, namely that boys will only like me if I am mysterious (never worked, p.s.), being clear, open, loving, caring, and on the same page with those you love, respect, and care about will change your life.

The pain of a relationship that you desperately want to work and to be super strong is real. It can become a real headache, literally, to try to be perfect for someone who just won't reciprocate. Where coming home from a stressful day just turns into an even more stressful day because you two don't have the tools necessary to talk things through. Or one person tries to fix it, when the other person is just trying to vent. Or one person needs completely separate time with zero contact for a little while, and the other feels abandoned. These feelings are completely normal.

Have you ever before seen folks with such a deep connection that they don't have to communicate using words? A relationship where each partner could almost predict how their partner would be feeling, what they might need, and what would make their day better? Building such a close relationship is absolutely doable. It's just a matter of better understanding how to approach your partner, establishing a mutual language of safety, support, and love, and scheduling time to practice this language.

Ultimately, the strength of your relationship will depend on the habits that you two developed toward one another. What do you do as soon as your partner comes home, if anything? How do you let them know you're hurting? Or happy? Or sad? Do you two regularly schedule dates? What are some of the other person's favorite things that never fail to cheer them up? How often do you initiate some of those favorite things of theirs? Just as brushing your teeth is (hopefully) one of the first things you do each morning, read on to learn exactly what items to block off on your calendar to establish some habits that will strengthen and help weather-proof your relationship.

30 Day Challenge

What's this 30-day challenge going to look like? There are going to be four rules, and you are going to review the rules first thing every morning and last thing every evening. In fact, I recommend getting out your phone right now and taking a picture of these 4 rules, then making the picture one of your favorites.

Here are the four rules:

1. Schedule Daily Dedicated Time to Speak
2. Commit to Weekly Relationship Review
3. Always Have a Call to Action When Fighting
4. Be Willing to Compromise

I'll be diving into these four rules in far more detail in the pages to follow. In the meantime, I really want you thinking about these concepts and about how you can apply them to your life unapologetically, and in a way that meshes with who you are, and who you want to be. But before you do that, there's one more step.

Which relationships do you want to work on? Maybe the one with your partner? Your best friend? Your best friend from ages ago with whom you lost touch sometime over the last four to fourteen years? Your mom? Your boss? Your best/worst employee? Pick one or two relationships on which to focus over the next thirty days. And commit, right here and right now, to seeing this challenge to its end. Even on the hard days. Especially on the easy days when you don't think you need it anymore. 30 days can truly fly. Let's fly together, and emerge stronger and with far more fulfilling, open, honest relationships on the other side.

Here's what you'll need. First, you'll have to have an open, honest conversation with your one or two people about the fact that you would like to strengthen your relationship, and ask if they are open to trying the challenge out together, with you leading the way. Getting their buy-in is super important. We are not looking to manipulate. Second, once you get their buy-in, schedule a specific time of day that's as consistent as possible for you two to speak. In person, as often as possible, is best. If that doesn't work each time, schedule a video call. If that won't work either, a call would be ok. Most importantly: stick it in your calendar. Then, make it a daily calendar entry. Third, pick your day and time for your weekly relationship review. Pop it in your calendar. Finally, put rules three and four in your back pocket for when you'll need them.

You are going to fall off the wagon sometimes. That's not only ok, but it's expected. The key is to just to get back on track and try again the next day. Each day is a new day and a fresh start. I ask for you to commit to trying each day. To roll with the punches and if you don't precisely get it right one day, you agree to try to do better the next. No beating yourself up allowed.

Finally, get out a piece of paper and a pen and write these rules down, preferably on two sheets of paper. One sheet will go on the fridge, right at eye level, and the other will join you at work, displayed someplace that you often look, right next to you on your table, perhaps. Next, decide today, right now, that you'll be reading this list first thing each morning, preferably out loud. By doing so, you are recommitting to this challenge, and to strengthening your relationship.

Let's get started.

RULE 1: SCHEDULE DEDICATED TIME TO SPEAK

"Leona, tell me the truth. Are you working so much longer every night because you don't want to spend time with me?" Talk about a metaphorical punch to the gut. It was year one of my matrimonial law firm, and I felt I had to put in the crazy hours to make the dream work. But the dream included the perfect life with my husband, who was now telling me in no uncertain terms that my actions were making him feel pretty low on the Leona list of priorities. My husband is my best friend. He has been since basically date one. I adore spending time with him and had absolutely no idea that my longer hours building the firm were making him feel that way. We had a really good solution-packed chat, and I began coming home far earlier so we could have "us" time. In fact, as soon as either of us gets home from work, we ensure that we speak right away.

At what time of day would you be most receptive to a talk? If you're moodier first thing in the morning, then that probably shouldn't be the dedicated time to chat. If you get burnt out right after work, that wouldn't be the best time. As bedtime nears, do you become solely focused on bed? Maybe don't pick right before bedtime. My husband and I look to chat as soon as both of us get home from work. A successful couple I know does "wine o'clock" each early evening on their deck, over a glass of wine and a spectacular view. Coffee time is a great time. My accountability partner and I check in literally first thing in the morning as soon as we're up. My coach hears from me around mealtimes and after each cup of water.

What to chat about. This part actually, is far less important. You guys can chat about literally anything, so long as it is bringing you closer together. Some places to start are asking them about their day. Or what they ate for breakfast and lunch. Or something you know happened that day. The key is to make this time and to give them your undivided attention.

Full attention is key. There is nothing more frustrating than having to constantly compete for the attention of someone who is important to you. So put the phone away. Don't tune them out. Don't think about your to do list or what's for dinner. Actively listen to what they're saying, even if, as they're telling you about their day, you don't fully understand the complexities of what they did. Be curious. Ask questions. The goal is simply time together, to talk about anything and everything. Let them vent. Let them be excited. Let them share their frustrations and joys and worries. Your job is to actively be there. Just make sure it's a back and forth conversation, and that neither one of you are doing all the talking.

Greet this person with enthusiasm. Presumably, you want to grow closer to them, so show it! Think about your tone. You've finally got time for both of you two to just be together. You want this. Make clear through your words, inflection, expression, and attitude that you are excited. There's nothing worse than showing up to spend time with someone you really like, and they don't really seem to care. It just doesn't feel good. On the other hand, don't overdo it. Being genuine is key, so really focus on why you want to strengthen your relationship with this person, and then bring that attitude with you.

This is not an opportunity to complain about the other person. Don't do it. There'll be time to discuss things that could have gone better and strategize exactly what measures to put in place to ensure that it never happens again. Here's an opportunity, every single day, to grow closer to this person, not have daily opportunities to bring them down. Don't be that person.

They say that time is our most precious commodity. It's tempting, especially when we are stressed out, to revert to behaviors that led you to decide to read this chapter in the first place. Do you jump straight on the phone with someone else to talk through what went on in your day? Turn the tv on? Scroll through social media? Put on the headphones and block out your world, including the very person with whom you are trying to strengthen your relationship? Right now, literally block off that daily time in your calendar to spend with them. What to talk about? After all, the big things tend not to change day to day. First, commit to listening actively. No multitasking, no mindlessly uh-huhing your way through the conversation. Instead, tell yourself to lean in, to actively listen and use terms such as, "what happened next," "how did that make you feel," "got it," etc. To get the conversation started, first think about what time of day you are having this conversation. If you two are speaking first thing in the morning, consider asking about how they slept, whether they had any dreams, how they feel, what the plan is for the day, and what time they plan on getting home. If it's during a break at work, consider asking about how their day is going, how motivated they are feeling, what their plan is for the rest of the day, and what they had or will be having for lunch. If you two are speaking after work, consider asking questions about how their day went, how they are feeling, what they ate, and how they'd like to unwind.

It's ok if you don't know or understand the full details of the work that they are working on. That's not the point. The point is that you care enough to ask. You are taking the initiative to show curiosity and are taking interest in something that they do for a decent chunk of their day. Think of this as bringing you two closer together. Try your best to engage and hear your person as they are explaining what is important to them. Do your best not to yawn or look around as the other person is speaking. Instead, look at them and really try to understand what they are saying.

Another important thing to ask, especially when you begin to feel the itch to solve the other person's problems and make them feel better on rougher days is whether they are asking for help, or whether they just need to vent. One of the worst things in a conversation is when one person just wants to get something painful off their chest, and the other person immediately chips in with a detailed action plan, uninvited. The first person often feels as though they weren't heard, even though the second person is showing that they really did listen, and even came up with a beautiful solution to boot! Then, consider establishing a code phrase that each of you can use to immediately let the other person know whether one of you is just looking to vent, and is just seeking support and understanding, or whether one of you is seeking help or advice.

What do you do if you skip a day? Or can't do the dedicated time to which you two committed to speaking? Pick a different time that day, if possible. If it's not possible, let them know that you'd like to speak at another time, if possible. Let them know that you're sorry that you won't be able to make it, why it is you won't be able to make it, to when you'd like to reschedule, and that you are committed to continuing the daily communication. Communicating that you won't be able to make it, but that this is still important to you, is key. Also, try not to make a habit of skipping communication time. If the time that you two picked is no longer working for you, discuss changing it to a different time going forward.

RULE 2: COMMIT TO WEEKLY RELATIONSHIP REVIEW

Remember when you and this person really hit it off? When times were amazing, and there was no question that the good outweighed the bad. The great times almost sparkled, they felt so good. But after a while, the formerly sparkly became normal. You and your partner stopped trying quite as hard, at least on a daily basis, because you two began to feel so comfortable around one another. With comfort comes letting things hang out a little more, so to speak. Since we are no longer constantly on our best behavior once things get comfortable, it's easy for fights to crop up more often, and for resentments and little hurts to build up. Often, when the little things have built up past a certain level, folks tend to either distance themselves or blow up, ironically usually over one more little thing that, by itself, would likely be pretty insignificant. Totally normal.

Have you ever been on the receiving end of hearing all of the ways that you let another person down since you were two years old? Been there, and it usually feels pretty unfair, especially if the bulk of the repeated complaints are about things that happened at least a decade ago. But the fact is, the hurt remains, and sometimes festers, especially if the other person never felt heard or felt as though you were committed to changing so what happened doesn't happen again. Relationship review should help a lot with this.

Do you and your partner have an easy time of complaining at and possibly even yelling at one another when the other does something wrong, but difficulty figuring out how to fix it for the future? Blowing up is easy. We're wired to do so from birth, to let mom know when we're hungry, or when we've pooped our diaper. However, blowing up without making a plan for how to do things differently is recipe for increased friction in your relationship. Relationship review will give you a weekly place to not only share what hasn't been going well, but how to work together to make a plan so that it never happens again.

So, what is relationship review, anyway? It's a weekly conversation comprised of three parts. First, you two thank each other for all of the ways the other person went above and beyond that week. Second, each of you talks about what could have gone better. Third, each of you discuss what you two will do going forward so that the things that went wrong won't ever happen again.

Thank the Other Person for Ways They Went Above and Beyond Over the Past Week

Thanking each other should be a sincere, thoughtful exercise. You should not be turning into a Toy Story Woody doll, mindlessly listing the same things over and over to the point that what you are saying loses meaning. Instead, really think about what the other person did that week and give them shoutouts about those things they did that really made you feel good. Did they do chores that you typically hate? Or a chore that is normally your responsibility? Something sweet they did first thing in the morning, such as making you coffee or tea, or getting you water? Something they did while you were at work? Something related to the kids? Something they took care of right before or as you got home from work? Something before bedtime?

We control what it is that filters up to our consciousness. By engaging in this portion of relationship review, you two are each training your brains to focus on the good, the stuff that is working, the things for which you are now accountable for sharing each week. Now instead of fixating on your partner's clothes strewn around the bedroom, or the fact that they keep the toilet seat up all the time, or their traipsing around the house in their outside shoes, you get to keep an active eye out for the good they do.

A typical gratitude portion that I share with my husband may look something like this:

Thank you so much for:
- Making delicious dinners all week long;
- Spicing up our food just right;
- Making delicious mocktails that totally scratch the after-dinner itch;
- Throwing out the garbage;
- Taking down the recyclables;
- Vacuuming;
- Helping make our home look perfect for our guests;
- Cleaning the bathrooms;

- Making perfect coffee that's got the perfect amount of milk and honey in it and bringing it to me in the mornings;

- Saving amazing biscuits with fixings from dinner you got yourself, so we could enjoy them together on Saturday morning;

- Confiding in me about things that are bothering you;

- Being comfortable with me spending a few nights this past week with networking dinners and events;

- Letting me come to you and share the hard stuff about work;

- Being the best advice-giver when it comes to putting in policies and procedures to keep the same mistakes from ever happening again in my company;

- For immediately knowing where on my neck and shoulders and back to massage to make the pain go away;

- For the very best hugs and snuggles that take the stress away;

- For kisses;

- For taking the train with me once this week;

- For tons of cuddles on Saturday morning;

- For helping me set up my offices in the new space;

- For being the very best uncle ever, and making our niece feel so comfortable and happy;

- For being a wonderful brother in law and making our sister in law feel so comfortable leaving their baby with us; and

- For being my everything after one heck of a stressful week!

A typical gratitude that my husband might share with me might look like:

Thank you:

- For making sure that we get breakfast;

- For being better about going to sleep early some nights;

- For doing dishes;

- For asking about my family and making sure I have a good relationship with them;

- For being wonderful to your family;

- For making me tea;

- And complimenting my coffee most days;

- For making me so comfortable that I get sleepy near you;

- For starting to unpack your clothing, even if your unpacking process is to move them from one place to another place to a third place;

- For buying delicious chocolate for us to share;

- For telling me about your day and listening to my advice about any issues you might have, whether big or small;

- For making sure I'm drinking enough water and buying more water;

- For going through the mail and cleaning the table, even though you needed to invite people to our house to do that;

- For ordering the Green Chef foods after you had accidentally canceled them;

- For making sure that I'm adequately warm or cool or in between, as needed;

- For putting away some of the dishes from the dishwasher after they are clean;

- For liking the vegetarian food, and for making sure that as we are trying to be healthier, you are supporting that;

- For being more communicative with me when you're staying out late; and

- For asking about my day.

There are no correct things to be grateful for. The key is to be sincere and specific. Don't say things you don't mean just to keep your partner happy. Sincerity can be heard and felt, and we want the other person to see and hear and feel how invested you are. Also, don't be self-conscious about the things you are grateful for that you share with your partner. I'm regularly amazed by the sorts of things my husband picks up on and shares that he is grateful for. Often the smallest, most inconsequential things that I did just because, are the things that really touch him, and that he mentions during relationship review each week. The bringing me coffee in bed thing is pretty new, and he did it once, just because, and I loved it so much that it stuck. It brings me immense pleasure that he goes out of his way not only to wake up sometimes hours earlier than he needs to in order to ensure that I get some coffee, grind the beans, make the coffee, mix it right, and bring it to me, and makes the start to my day that much better. In turn, he usually has a huge grin on his face when he sees how excited I am that I get coffee in bed that he brings to me, and that he gets to make me feel that way.

Share what Could Have Gone Better Over the Past Week

The next part is the what could have gone better portion. Here's the chance to be vulnerable and really let the other person know what bothered you, made you feel not great, and share in a safe place. First though, you and your partner have to commit to not freaking out at one another. The whole purpose of this part is to be open and make improvements together, not to make one another feel worse. This is a safe place, where sharing is not only allowed, but expected. It's the designated place each week to bring this stuff up if you two didn't have an opportunity to discuss whatever it is during the week. But the safety has to be assured or this will not work.

Also, this is a place to discuss things that went wrong, specific incidents that occurred or didn't occur. What this is not an opportunity to do is attack the other person's character. For instance, do not, under any circumstances, call your partner lazy. Instead, consider mentioning that it hurt your feelings that the other person did not take out the garbage, especially since you cooked and cleaned and did the laundry that week. Don't call them high-strung, but instead, mention that the time your partner started screaming and breaking dishes made you feel terrible and powerless. Don't call them aloof, tell them that you didn't feel you could come to them when your boss yelled at you for something that wasn't your fault, because you weren't sure how they would respond, if at all. Don't call them spoiled, tell them how it really hurt your feelings when you found four new pairs of shoes and the receipt, and they didn't say a word to you about the purchases. In short, do not mention adjectives or characteristics or what the other person is like. Instead really try to zero in on one or more specific incidents or omissions that occurred over the last week that bothered you.

Here are examples that my husband and I shared with one another during relationship reviews:

Me: I really didn't like when we had that argument and you gave me the silent treatment and fell asleep right away before we talked about it and resolved it. I couldn't sleep for hours and was super anxious and stressed and upset, especially since you lay there happily snoring while I couldn't even sleep.

My Husband: I didn't like that we had planned to have dinner at a certain time when you told me you'd be coming home, and then, instead of telling me that you were planning to stay late to network, you said that you would be just a little longer, then thirty minutes later said you were almost done, then thirty minutes later didn't pick up the phone when I called you, and so you ended up coming home two hours later. It was too late for me to eat, especially since you know that I don't like eating late, and it was too late for me to order anything.

But Leona, what if I don't like sharing what seems to be inconsequential things with the other person? To some people, this form of communication is completely new. That's normal. There will be a learning curve. Here's the thing, however: you deserve more than just keeping quiet anytime and every time your partner does something that you don't like. Because even if it doesn't feel like it right now, the little, tiny things are adding up inside, and even if they feel insignificant individually, each serves as a small brick to create a bigger and bigger wall between you two. This wall will serve to create distance between you two and will push you away from them. Let's keep this wall from forming in the first place, or if part of it has already been built from the little things, let's work to knock it down.

So, how to do this. Keep active watch during the week about things the other person does that hurts your feelings. Write it down, even if it really seems like something silly or frivolous. Try not to blow up, unless the issue is something that is emergency-level or otherwise immediately requires you to discuss it with your partner. Think of framing it as [this specific action or inaction that happened over the past week] made me feel [how it made you feel]. Be honest, be prepared to be vulnerable, and get ready to feel way closer to your partner.

Make a Plan for What Needs to Change to Ensure that the Things that Could Have Gone Better Never Happen Again (aka Rules 3 and 4)

Bringing up what could have gone better over the last week is an important start, but the true meat and potatoes of fixing things lies in step three: making a plan together for what needs to change to ensure that the things that could have gone better never happen again. This portion will require input from both of you.

First, you want to make sure that you clearly understood what it was that was bothering the other person. When I came home late from work without telling my husband exactly when I would be coming home from work, he wasn't mad that I was networking. We didn't mind at all that I was working late to improve my business and establish trust with folks who could really help me grow my practice. He did not care what time I was coming home, per se. What really bothered him was that I did not communicate what time I would be coming home and had told him I would be able to make it home for dinner and then got home after 9:00 pm. It was the lack of my communication regarding what time I would be getting home, and also whether or not we would be eating dinner together, that hurt his feelings. He was also pretty worried when he didn't hear from me well after the time I said I would be home. I stated my version of the above to make sure I really understood what he was telling me, and then we zeroed in on the fact that it was 1) my lack of communication and 2) my making plans with my husband, namely, to have dinner together that didn't end up happening that caused the hurt feelings. We then made a plan that, going forward, I would text my husband if I planned to be out later than anticipated, and to also let him know in advance if I was planning to be out during the time that we normally eat dinner. In fact, since this conversation, we have made it a point to share what time we anticipate coming home that evening each morning. I am definitely the more social of us, and so if I have any plans, I share those with my husband in the morning. If something comes up during the day where I will have to stay late, I text my husband letting him know approximately when I will be coming home, and that I will let him know as soon as I'm done and am heading home. I also let my husband know when I'm on my way home each day, so he knows to expect me.

It is hard to hear criticism. As an honor-roller and high achiever, criticism from those closest to me always seemed to hit especially hard. However, I would recommend that you and your partner not think about this part of relationship review as criticism. Instead, it's an opportunity to keep growing closer together instead of building up resentment toward one another. This way, you two get to nip any almost inconsequential or not-so-inconsequential things in the bud, and make sure they never happen again. It's about listening to one another and looking to be better for them, and vice versa. When you two first started dating, it was so much easier to share preferences and likes and dislikes. The goal back then was to really please the other person all the time. This is just like that, even if it may be a few, or even many years since you two first dated. Think of this as being a team with the other person, problem solving together to make things better for one another.

RULE 3: ALWAYS HAVE A CALL TO ACTION WHEN FIGHTING

Disagreements will come up, and relationship review will be a great time to tackle them. The biggest thing to remember is that the goal to resolving fights effectively is to fix it, not just yell and scream and break things or silent treatment the other person until you two snap out of it. The focus should be to first, identify the issue or issues, then discuss precisely what those issues are, focusing on the exact action or inaction that occurred, and how it made you feel, then work together to come to a solution together so this fight will be your last on this issue. As mentioned in the part two of relationship review, try using the following sentence to frame what hurt your feelings: [this specific action or inaction] made me feel [how it made you feel].

When fighting, do your best not to drag in the past, unless it directly relates, perhaps in the form of repeated behavior this time around. What happened seven years ago will not help you two get to the call to action and resolution; bringing up the past in a way whose purpose is solely to add fuel to the fire will only serve to drive you two further apart, instead of help you two get closer together. Let the past stay in the past, especially when it comes to fights.

Emotions are great at getting in the way of rational thinking and planning. When you're mad, you sometimes may not want to fix it right then. You may want to vent, or get it out of your system, before tackling it head-on in a constructive way with your partner. So, get the venting out of your system, just not with your partner. Go to the gym, hit a punching bag a few times, call a friend, and once you are thinking clearly again, sit down with your partner to discuss what happened.

The key is to work together to come up with solutions that work for both of you, long-term, instead of one person capitulating to the other.

RULE 4: BE WILLING TO COMPROMISE

Compromise sometimes stinks. When we're four, and we really want the ice cream before dinner, we are not looking for a compromise. When I'm at the store looking for a specific pair of pants, I'm not looking to compromise, either. But in order for a relationship to grow and to succeed, it's all about meeting your person in the middle. Sometimes they will "get their way," and sometimes you will, but there needs to be a give and take.

So, how to do it? First, listen to what it is the other person wants, or share what you want, and really be open to listening to their response. Consider phrasing it as "I would like to _____. What do you think?" Next, give them the chance to respond. No ultimatums. No tone that suggests that it'll be your way or the highway. What do you both want? Be ready to respect the other person's wishes in finding middle ground.

Recently, I wanted to spend a Saturday having adventures outside in New York City with my husband. He was really craving a stay-at-home day together, complete with movies and the comfort of our couch. We compromised by agreeing upon a time to go grab a meal outdoors that we walked to and from and spent the rest of the day snuggled up unwinding. The compromise scratched both of our itches. That is what you should be aiming for any time you and your partner do not agree.

Honesty is truly the best policy when it comes to explaining why it is you want what you want. Be ready to be vulnerable. Also, be ready to explain why it is you want what you want, besides that you want it, darn it. What would it mean to you to get your way? What part of it are you willing to give up, and still be reasonably happy? What would you be open to doing instead that will still keep you pretty happy? Working together to figure out what solution will leave you both satisfied will help you two become closer and closer over time.

About the Author

Leona S. Krasner, Esq., MBA, first became interested in relationships and justice at the age of seven, when she decided to become an attorney. As she studied the Social Sciences, her major at Brooklyn Technical High School, and then went on to double major in Psychology and Politics at New York University, her interest in relationships and justice only grew. Her studies at Washington and Lee University School of Law, where she earned her Juris Doctorate, and then at the Stern School of Business at New York University, where she earned her Master's of Business Administration, shaped her decision to pursue the law, and then start her own law firm. Today, Leona is the Managing Partner of Krasner Law, PLLC, a family law firm that helps folks in New York and New Jersey get married, stop being married, and help with the children, too. Her boutique law firm is quickly expanding, and she currently has twelve employees. When not assisting clients with their family law issues, Leona regularly posts relationship tips across social media. Her ideology is that she would love to help people strengthen their relationships, if at all possible. If that doesn't work, she and her firm stand ready to assist.

When not practicing law, Leona helps students as Managing Director of Krasner Review, LLC, a tutoring company that assists students with standardized examination preparation, application preparation, and scholarship negotiation. She also enjoys managing and performing at concerts that she puts on as Managing Director of her nonprofit organization, Tunes for Tots & Teens, through which volunteer musicians play concerts for children. She also enjoys going on adventures with her husband, traveling, and reading.

Contact Information
Leona Krasner, Esq., MBA
Company: Krasner Law, PLLC
Email: leona@lkrasner.com
LinkedIn: www.linkedin.com/in/leonakrasner
Facebook: www.facebook.com/leonakrasner
Website: www.lkrasner.com

Conclusion

Taking-Action, is the most important step towards success. The simple truth is that dreams, visions and goals are achieved and accomplished only through action. None of the theories and plans will work if you don't take any action.

DREAM IT, THINK IT, PLAN IT, THEN DO IT.

Execution is the secret ingredient many people can have the same idea but what sets them apart is how they execute it.

Often times someone is not sure about the best direction to take to implement their dreams and therefore the temptation is to wait until the entire road map is available or the timing is perfect in order to begin.

So, it becomes a waiting game, waiting until all the pieces of the puzzle are available and make sense, waiting for the right conditions and circumstances, waiting and breeding procrastination upon procrastination – a procrastination infestation, over analyzing and saying that I will do it one day.

Start at the level where you are, then grow and increase your skill level and output over time. Do something. Inaction is a killer of big dreams.

The reality is that if you don't take-action to pursue
your dreams nobody will do it for you.

Month		Year	

SUNDAY ○	MONDAY ○	TUESDAY ○	WEDNESDAY ○
6am	6am	6am	6am
7am	7am	7am	7am
8am	8am	8am	8am
9am	9am	9am	9am
10am	10am	10am	10am
11am	11am	11am	11am
12pm	12pm	12pm	12pm
1pm	1pm	1pm	1pm
2pm	2pm	2pm	2pm
3pm	3pm	3pm	3pm
4pm	4pm	4pm	4pm
5pm	5pm	5pm	5pm
6pm	6pm	6pm	6pm
7pm	7pm	7pm	7pm
8pm	8pm	8pm	8pm
9pm	9pm	9pm	9pm
10pm	10pm	10pm	10pm
11pm	11pm	11pm	11pm
12pm	12pm	12pm	12pm

"Optimism is the faith that leads to achievement."
– Helen Keller

THURSDAY	⭘	FRIDAY	⭘	SATURDAY	⭘
6am		6am		6am	
7am		7am		7am	
8am		8am		8am	
9am		9am		9am	
10am		10am		10am	
11am		11am		11am	
12pm		12pm		12pm	
1pm		1pm		1pm	
2pm		2pm		2pm	
3pm		3pm		3pm	
4pm		4pm		4pm	
5pm		5pm		5pm	
6pm		6pm		6pm	
7pm		7pm		7pm	
8pm		8pm		8pm	
9pm		9pm		9pm	
10pm		10pm		10pm	
11pm		11pm		11pm	
12pm		12pm		12pm	

Wheel of Life

To-do

Reflections

Notes

Quotations & Tips

POWERFUL WOMEN TODAY

Month [   ]   Year [   ]

SUNDAY ●		MONDAY ●		TUESDAY ●		WEDNESDAY ●
6am		6am		6am		6am
7am		7am		7am		7am
8am		8am		8am		8am
9am		9am		9am		9am
10am		10am		10am		10am
11am		11am		11am		11am
12pm		12pm		12pm		12pm
1pm		1pm		1pm		1pm
2pm		2pm		2pm		2pm
3pm		3pm		3pm		3pm
4pm		4pm		4pm		4pm
5pm		5pm		5pm		5pm
6pm		6pm		6pm		6pm
7pm		7pm		7pm		7pm
8pm		8pm		8pm		8pm
9pm		9pm		9pm		9pm
10pm		10pm		10pm		10pm
11pm		11pm		11pm		11pm
12pm		12pm		12pm		12pm

WEEKLY CHECK INS

THURSDAY		FRIDAY		SATURDAY	
6am		6am		6am	
7am		7am		7am	
8am		8am		8am	
9am		9am		9am	
10am		10am		10am	
11am		11am		11am	
12pm		12pm		12pm	
1pm		1pm		1pm	
2pm		2pm		2pm	
3pm		3pm		3pm	
4pm		4pm		4pm	
5pm		5pm		5pm	
6pm		6pm		6pm	
7pm		7pm		7pm	
8pm		8pm		8pm	
9pm		9pm		9pm	
10pm		10pm		10pm	
11pm		11pm		11pm	
12pm		12pm		12pm	

Wheel of Life

To-do

Reflections

Notes

Quotations & Tips

POWERFUL WOMEN TODAY

Month		Year	

SUNDAY ●	MONDAY ●	TUESDAY ●	WEDNESDAY ●
6am	6am	6am	6am
7am	7am	7am	7am
8am	8am	8am	8am
9am	9am	9am	9am
10am	10am	10am	10am
11am	11am	11am	11am
12pm	12pm	12pm	12pm
1pm	1pm	1pm	1pm
2pm	2pm	2pm	2pm
3pm	3pm	3pm	3pm
4pm	4pm	4pm	4pm
5pm	5pm	5pm	5pm
6pm	6pm	6pm	6pm
7pm	7pm	7pm	7pm
8pm	8pm	8pm	8pm
9pm	9pm	9pm	9pm
10pm	10pm	10pm	10pm
11pm	11pm	11pm	11pm
12pm	12pm	12pm	12pm

"Make the most of yourself by fanning the tiny, inner sparks of possibility into flames of achievement." – *Golda Meir*

THURSDAY ○		FRIDAY ○		SATURDAY ○	
6am		6am		6am	
7am		7am		7am	
8am		8am		8am	
9am		9am		9am	
10am		10am		10am	
11am		11am		11am	
12pm		12pm		12pm	
1pm		1pm		1pm	
2pm		2pm		2pm	
3pm		3pm		3pm	
4pm		4pm		4pm	
5pm		5pm		5pm	
6pm		6pm		6pm	
7pm		7pm		7pm	
8pm		8pm		8pm	
9pm		9pm		9pm	
10pm		10pm		10pm	
11pm		11pm		11pm	
12pm		12pm		12pm	

Wheel of Life

To-do

Reflections

Notes

Quotations & Tips

POWERFUL WOMEN TODAY

Month [   ]   Year [   ]

SUNDAY ⬤		MONDAY ⬤		TUESDAY ⬤		WEDNESDAY ⬤	
6am		6am		6am		6am	
7am		7am		7am		7am	
8am		8am		8am		8am	
9am		9am		9am		9am	
10am		10am		10am		10am	
11am		11am		11am		11am	
12pm		12pm		12pm		12pm	
1pm		1pm		1pm		1pm	
2pm		2pm		2pm		2pm	
3pm		3pm		3pm		3pm	
4pm		4pm		4pm		4pm	
5pm		5pm		5pm		5pm	
6pm		6pm		6pm		6pm	
7pm		7pm		7pm		7pm	
8pm		8pm		8pm		8pm	
9pm		9pm		9pm		9pm	
10pm		10pm		10pm		10pm	
11pm		11pm		11pm		11pm	
12pm		12pm		12pm		12pm	

"Knowing what must be done does away with fear."
— Rosa Parks

THURSDAY	⬤	FRIDAY	⬤	SATURDAY	⬤
6am		6am		6am	
7am		7am		7am	
8am		8am		8am	
9am		9am		9am	
10am		10am		10am	
11am		11am		11am	
12pm		12pm		12pm	
1pm		1pm		1pm	
2pm		2pm		2pm	
3pm		3pm		3pm	
4pm		4pm		4pm	
5pm		5pm		5pm	
6pm		6pm		6pm	
7pm		7pm		7pm	
8pm		8pm		8pm	
9pm		9pm		9pm	
10pm		10pm		10pm	
11pm		11pm		11pm	
12pm		12pm		12pm	

Wheel of Life

To-do

Reflections

Notes

Quotations & Tips

POWERFUL
WOMEN TODAY

Month			Year	

SUNDAY	●	MONDAY	●	TUESDAY	●	WEDNESDAY	●
6am		6am		6am		6am	
7am		7am		7am		7am	
8am		8am		8am		8am	
9am		9am		9am		9am	
10am		10am		10am		10am	
11am		11am		11am		11am	
12pm		12pm		12pm		12pm	
1pm		1pm		1pm		1pm	
2pm		2pm		2pm		2pm	
3pm		3pm		3pm		3pm	
4pm		4pm		4pm		4pm	
5pm		5pm		5pm		5pm	
6pm		6pm		6pm		6pm	
7pm		7pm		7pm		7pm	
8pm		8pm		8pm		8pm	
9pm		9pm		9pm		9pm	
10pm		10pm		10pm		10pm	
11pm		11pm		11pm		11pm	
12pm		12pm		12pm		12pm	

> *"I didn't get there by wishing for it or hoping for it, but by working for it."* — *Estée Lauder*

THURSDAY	⬤	FRIDAY	⬤	SATURDAY	⬤
6am		6am		6am	
7am		7am		7am	
8am		8am		8am	
9am		9am		9am	
10am		10am		10am	
11am		11am		11am	
12pm		12pm		12pm	
1pm		1pm		1pm	
2pm		2pm		2pm	
3pm		3pm		3pm	
4pm		4pm		4pm	
5pm		5pm		5pm	
6pm		6pm		6pm	
7pm		7pm		7pm	
8pm		8pm		8pm	
9pm		9pm		9pm	
10pm		10pm		10pm	
11pm		11pm		11pm	
12pm		12pm		12pm	

Wheel of Life

To-do

Reflections

Notes

Quotations & Tips

POWERFUL WOMEN TODAY

| Month | | Year | |

SUNDAY	○	MONDAY	○	TUESDAY	○	WEDNESDAY	○
6am		6am		6am		6am	
7am		7am		7am		7am	
8am		8am		8am		8am	
9am		9am		9am		9am	
10am		10am		10am		10am	
11am		11am		11am		11am	
12pm		12pm		12pm		12pm	
1pm		1pm		1pm		1pm	
2pm		2pm		2pm		2pm	
3pm		3pm		3pm		3pm	
4pm		4pm		4pm		4pm	
5pm		5pm		5pm		5pm	
6pm		6pm		6pm		6pm	
7pm		7pm		7pm		7pm	
8pm		8pm		8pm		8pm	
9pm		9pm		9pm		9pm	
10pm		10pm		10pm		10pm	
11pm		11pm		11pm		11pm	
12pm		12pm		12pm		12pm	

> *"Power's not given to you. You have to take it."*
> *— Beyoncé Knowles Carter*

WEEKLY
CHECK INS

THURSDAY	⭘	FRIDAY	⭘	SATURDAY	⭘
6am		6am		6am	
7am		7am		7am	
8am		8am		8am	
9am		9am		9am	
10am		10am		10am	
11am		11am		11am	
12pm		12pm		12pm	
1pm		1pm		1pm	
2pm		2pm		2pm	
3pm		3pm		3pm	
4pm		4pm		4pm	
5pm		5pm		5pm	
6pm		6pm		6pm	
7pm		7pm		7pm	
8pm		8pm		8pm	
9pm		9pm		9pm	
10pm		10pm		10pm	
11pm		11pm		11pm	
12pm		12pm		12pm	

Wheel of Life

To-do

Reflections

Notes

Quotations & Tips

POWERFUL WOMEN TODAY

Month		Year	

SUNDAY ⬤	MONDAY ⬤	TUESDAY ⬤	WEDNESDAY ⬤
6am	6am	6am	6am
7am	7am	7am	7am
8am	8am	8am	8am
9am	9am	9am	9am
10am	10am	10am	10am
11am	11am	11am	11am
12pm	12pm	12pm	12pm
1pm	1pm	1pm	1pm
2pm	2pm	2pm	2pm
3pm	3pm	3pm	3pm
4pm	4pm	4pm	4pm
5pm	5pm	5pm	5pm
6pm	6pm	6pm	6pm
7pm	7pm	7pm	7pm
8pm	8pm	8pm	8pm
9pm	9pm	9pm	9pm
10pm	10pm	10pm	10pm
11pm	11pm	11pm	11pm
12pm	12pm	12pm	12pm

"The most difficult thing is the decision to act,
the rest is merely tenacity." — *Amelia Earhart*

THURSDAY	⬤	FRIDAY	⬤	SATURDAY	⬤
6am		6am		6am	
7am		7am		7am	
8am		8am		8am	
9am		9am		9am	
10am		10am		10am	
11am		11am		11am	
12pm		12pm		12pm	
1pm		1pm		1pm	
2pm		2pm		2pm	
3pm		3pm		3pm	
4pm		4pm		4pm	
5pm		5pm		5pm	
6pm		6pm		6pm	
7pm		7pm		7pm	
8pm		8pm		8pm	
9pm		9pm		9pm	
10pm		10pm		10pm	
11pm		11pm		11pm	
12pm		12pm		12pm	

Wheel of Life

To-do

Reflections

Notes

Quotations & Tips

POWERFUL
WOMEN TODAY

Month		Year	

SUNDAY ⚪	MONDAY ⚪	TUESDAY ⚪	WEDNESDAY ⚪
6am	6am	6am	6am
7am	7am	7am	7am
8am	8am	8am	8am
9am	9am	9am	9am
10am	10am	10am	10am
11am	11am	11am	11am
12pm	12pm	12pm	12pm
1pm	1pm	1pm	1pm
2pm	2pm	2pm	2pm
3pm	3pm	3pm	3pm
4pm	4pm	4pm	4pm
5pm	5pm	5pm	5pm
6pm	6pm	6pm	6pm
7pm	7pm	7pm	7pm
8pm	8pm	8pm	8pm
9pm	9pm	9pm	9pm
10pm	10pm	10pm	10pm
11pm	11pm	11pm	11pm
12pm	12pm	12pm	12pm

"You can waste your lives drawing lines. Or you can live your life crossing them." — *Shonda Rhimes*

THURSDAY	⬤	FRIDAY	⬤	SATURDAY	⬤
6am		6am		6am	
7am		7am		7am	
8am		8am		8am	
9am		9am		9am	
10am		10am		10am	
11am		11am		11am	
12pm		12pm		12pm	
1pm		1pm		1pm	
2pm		2pm		2pm	
3pm		3pm		3pm	
4pm		4pm		4pm	
5pm		5pm		5pm	
6pm		6pm		6pm	
7pm		7pm		7pm	
8pm		8pm		8pm	
9pm		9pm		9pm	
10pm		10pm		10pm	
11pm		11pm		11pm	
12pm		12pm		12pm	

Wheel of Life

To-do

Reflections

Notes

Quotations & Tips

POWERFUL WOMEN TODAY

Month		Year	

SUNDAY ⬤	MONDAY ⬤	TUESDAY ⬤	WEDNESDAY ⬤
6am	6am	6am	6am
7am	7am	7am	7am
8am	8am	8am	8am
9am	9am	9am	9am
10am	10am	10am	10am
11am	11am	11am	11am
12pm	12pm	12pm	12pm
1pm	1pm	1pm	1pm
2pm	2pm	2pm	2pm
3pm	3pm	3pm	3pm
4pm	4pm	4pm	4pm
5pm	5pm	5pm	5pm
6pm	6pm	6pm	6pm
7pm	7pm	7pm	7pm
8pm	8pm	8pm	8pm
9pm	9pm	9pm	9pm
10pm	10pm	10pm	10pm
11pm	11pm	11pm	11pm
12pm	12pm	12pm	12pm

"I'd rather regret the things I've done than regret the things I haven't done." – *Lucille Ball*

THURSDAY	⚪	FRIDAY	⚪	SATURDAY	⚪
6am		6am		6am	
7am		7am		7am	
8am		8am		8am	
9am		9am		9am	
10am		10am		10am	
11am		11am		11am	
12pm		12pm		12pm	
1pm		1pm		1pm	
2pm		2pm		2pm	
3pm		3pm		3pm	
4pm		4pm		4pm	
5pm		5pm		5pm	
6pm		6pm		6pm	
7pm		7pm		7pm	
8pm		8pm		8pm	
9pm		9pm		9pm	
10pm		10pm		10pm	
11pm		11pm		11pm	
12pm		12pm		12pm	

Wheel of Life

To-do

Reflections

Notes

Quotations & Tips

POWERFUL WOMEN TODAY

Month

Year

SUNDAY ○		MONDAY ○		TUESDAY ○		WEDNESDAY ○	
6am		6am		6am		6am	
7am		7am		7am		7am	
8am		8am		8am		8am	
9am		9am		9am		9am	
10am		10am		10am		10am	
11am		11am		11am		11am	
12pm		12pm		12pm		12pm	
1pm		1pm		1pm		1pm	
2pm		2pm		2pm		2pm	
3pm		3pm		3pm		3pm	
4pm		4pm		4pm		4pm	
5pm		5pm		5pm		5pm	
6pm		6pm		6pm		6pm	
7pm		7pm		7pm		7pm	
8pm		8pm		8pm		8pm	
9pm		9pm		9pm		9pm	
10pm		10pm		10pm		10pm	
11pm		11pm		11pm		11pm	
12pm		12pm		12pm		12pm	

WEEKLY
CHECK INS

THURSDAY ⬤		FRIDAY ⬤		SATURDAY ⬤	
6am		6am		6am	
7am		7am		7am	
8am		8am		8am	
9am		9am		9am	
10am		10am		10am	
11am		11am		11am	
12pm		12pm		12pm	
1pm		1pm		1pm	
2pm		2pm		2pm	
3pm		3pm		3pm	
4pm		4pm		4pm	
5pm		5pm		5pm	
6pm		6pm		6pm	
7pm		7pm		7pm	
8pm		8pm		8pm	
9pm		9pm		9pm	
10pm		10pm		10pm	
11pm		11pm		11pm	
12pm		12pm		12pm	

Wheel of Life

To-do

Reflections

Notes

Quotations & Tips

POWERFUL WOMEN TODAY

Month		Year	

SUNDAY ●	MONDAY ●	TUESDAY ●	WEDNESDAY ●
6am	6am	6am	6am
7am	7am	7am	7am
8am	8am	8am	8am
9am	9am	9am	9am
10am	10am	10am	10am
11am	11am	11am	11am
12pm	12pm	12pm	12pm
1pm	1pm	1pm	1pm
2pm	2pm	2pm	2pm
3pm	3pm	3pm	3pm
4pm	4pm	4pm	4pm
5pm	5pm	5pm	5pm
6pm	6pm	6pm	6pm
7pm	7pm	7pm	7pm
8pm	8pm	8pm	8pm
9pm	9pm	9pm	9pm
10pm	10pm	10pm	10pm
11pm	11pm	11pm	11pm
12pm	12pm	12pm	12pm

WEEKLY
CHECK INS

THURSDAY	⭕	FRIDAY	⭕	SATURDAY	⭕
6am		6am		6am	
7am		7am		7am	
8am		8am		8am	
9am		9am		9am	
10am		10am		10am	
11am		11am		11am	
12pm		12pm		12pm	
1pm		1pm		1pm	
2pm		2pm		2pm	
3pm		3pm		3pm	
4pm		4pm		4pm	
5pm		5pm		5pm	
6pm		6pm		6pm	
7pm		7pm		7pm	
8pm		8pm		8pm	
9pm		9pm		9pm	
10pm		10pm		10pm	
11pm		11pm		11pm	
12pm		12pm		12pm	

Wheel of Life

To-do

Reflections

Notes

Quotations & Tips

POWERFUL WOMEN TODAY

Month		Year	

SUNDAY ⬤	MONDAY ⬤	TUESDAY ⬤	WEDNESDAY ⬤
6am	6am	6am	6am
7am	7am	7am	7am
8am	8am	8am	8am
9am	9am	9am	9am
10am	10am	10am	10am
11am	11am	11am	11am
12pm	12pm	12pm	12pm
1pm	1pm	1pm	1pm
2pm	2pm	2pm	2pm
3pm	3pm	3pm	3pm
4pm	4pm	4pm	4pm
5pm	5pm	5pm	5pm
6pm	6pm	6pm	6pm
7pm	7pm	7pm	7pm
8pm	8pm	8pm	8pm
9pm	9pm	9pm	9pm
10pm	10pm	10pm	10pm
11pm	11pm	11pm	11pm
12pm	12pm	12pm	12pm

WEEKLY
CHECK INS

THURSDAY	⚪	FRIDAY	⚪	SATURDAY	⚪
6am		6am		6am	
7am		7am		7am	
8am		8am		8am	
9am		9am		9am	
10am		10am		10am	
11am		11am		11am	
12pm		12pm		12pm	
1pm		1pm		1pm	
2pm		2pm		2pm	
3pm		3pm		3pm	
4pm		4pm		4pm	
5pm		5pm		5pm	
6pm		6pm		6pm	
7pm		7pm		7pm	
8pm		8pm		8pm	
9pm		9pm		9pm	
10pm		10pm		10pm	
11pm		11pm		11pm	
12pm		12pm		12pm	

Wheel of Life

To-do

Reflections

Notes

Quotations & Tips

POWERFUL WOMEN TODAY

Month		Year	

SUNDAY ⚪	MONDAY ⚪	TUESDAY ⚪	WEDNESDAY ⚪
6am	6am	6am	6am
7am	7am	7am	7am
8am	8am	8am	8am
9am	9am	9am	9am
10am	10am	10am	10am
11am	11am	11am	11am
12pm	12pm	12pm	12pm
1pm	1pm	1pm	1pm
2pm	2pm	2pm	2pm
3pm	3pm	3pm	3pm
4pm	4pm	4pm	4pm
5pm	5pm	5pm	5pm
6pm	6pm	6pm	6pm
7pm	7pm	7pm	7pm
8pm	8pm	8pm	8pm
9pm	9pm	9pm	9pm
10pm	10pm	10pm	10pm
11pm	11pm	11pm	11pm
12pm	12pm	12pm	12pm

"You can't give up! If you give up, you're like everybody else.". – Chris Evert

THURSDAY	○	FRIDAY	○	SATURDAY	○
6am		6am		6am	
7am		7am		7am	
8am		8am		8am	
9am		9am		9am	
10am		10am		10am	
11am		11am		11am	
12pm		12pm		12pm	
1pm		1pm		1pm	
2pm		2pm		2pm	
3pm		3pm		3pm	
4pm		4pm		4pm	
5pm		5pm		5pm	
6pm		6pm		6pm	
7pm		7pm		7pm	
8pm		8pm		8pm	
9pm		9pm		9pm	
10pm		10pm		10pm	
11pm		11pm		11pm	
12pm		12pm		12pm	

Wheel of Life

To-do

Reflections

Notes

Quotations & Tips

POWERFUL WOMEN TODAY

Month _____ Year _____

SUNDAY ⬤		MONDAY ⬤		TUESDAY ⬤		WEDNESDAY ⬤	
6am		6am		6am		6am	
7am		7am		7am		7am	
8am		8am		8am		8am	
9am		9am		9am		9am	
10am		10am		10am		10am	
11am		11am		11am		11am	
12pm		12pm		12pm		12pm	
1pm		1pm		1pm		1pm	
2pm		2pm		2pm		2pm	
3pm		3pm		3pm		3pm	
4pm		4pm		4pm		4pm	
5pm		5pm		5pm		5pm	
6pm		6pm		6pm		6pm	
7pm		7pm		7pm		7pm	
8pm		8pm		8pm		8pm	
9pm		9pm		9pm		9pm	
10pm		10pm		10pm		10pm	
11pm		11pm		11pm		11pm	
12pm		12pm		12pm		12pm	

"Done is better than perfect." – *Sheryl Sandberg*

THURSDAY ○	FRIDAY ○	SATURDAY ○
6am	6am	6am
7am	7am	7am
8am	8am	8am
9am	9am	9am
10am	10am	10am
11am	11am	11am
12pm	12pm	12pm
1pm	1pm	1pm
2pm	2pm	2pm
3pm	3pm	3pm
4pm	4pm	4pm
5pm	5pm	5pm
6pm	6pm	6pm
7pm	7pm	7pm
8pm	8pm	8pm
9pm	9pm	9pm
10pm	10pm	10pm
11pm	11pm	11pm
12pm	12pm	12pm

WEEKLY
CHECK INS

Wheel of Life

To-do

Reflections

Notes

Quotations & Tips

POWERFUL
WOMEN TODAY

Month		Year	

SUNDAY ⚪	MONDAY ⚪	TUESDAY ⚪	WEDNESDAY ⚪
6am	6am	6am	6am
7am	7am	7am	7am
8am	8am	8am	8am
9am	9am	9am	9am
10am	10am	10am	10am
11am	11am	11am	11am
12pm	12pm	12pm	12pm
1pm	1pm	1pm	1pm
2pm	2pm	2pm	2pm
3pm	3pm	3pm	3pm
4pm	4pm	4pm	4pm
5pm	5pm	5pm	5pm
6pm	6pm	6pm	6pm
7pm	7pm	7pm	7pm
8pm	8pm	8pm	8pm
9pm	9pm	9pm	9pm
10pm	10pm	10pm	10pm
11pm	11pm	11pm	11pm
12pm	12pm	12pm	12pm

WEEKLY CHECK INS

THURSDAY	○	FRIDAY	○	SATURDAY	○
6am		6am		6am	
7am		7am		7am	
8am		8am		8am	
9am		9am		9am	
10am		10am		10am	
11am		11am		11am	
12pm		12pm		12pm	
1pm		1pm		1pm	
2pm		2pm		2pm	
3pm		3pm		3pm	
4pm		4pm		4pm	
5pm		5pm		5pm	
6pm		6pm		6pm	
7pm		7pm		7pm	
8pm		8pm		8pm	
9pm		9pm		9pm	
10pm		10pm		10pm	
11pm		11pm		11pm	
12pm		12pm		12pm	

Wheel of Life

To-do

Reflections

Notes

Quotations & Tips

POWERFUL WOMEN TODAY

Month		Year	

SUNDAY ●	MONDAY ●	TUESDAY ●	WEDNESDAY ●
6am	6am	6am	6am
7am	7am	7am	7am
8am	8am	8am	8am
9am	9am	9am	9am
10am	10am	10am	10am
11am	11am	11am	11am
12pm	12pm	12pm	12pm
1pm	1pm	1pm	1pm
2pm	2pm	2pm	2pm
3pm	3pm	3pm	3pm
4pm	4pm	4pm	4pm
5pm	5pm	5pm	5pm
6pm	6pm	6pm	6pm
7pm	7pm	7pm	7pm
8pm	8pm	8pm	8pm
9pm	9pm	9pm	9pm
10pm	10pm	10pm	10pm
11pm	11pm	11pm	11pm
12pm	12pm	12pm	12pm

"It took me quite a long time to develop a voice, and now that I have it, I am not going to be silent." – *Madeleine Albright*

THURSDAY	⬤	FRIDAY	⬤	SATURDAY	⬤
6am		6am		6am	
7am		7am		7am	
8am		8am		8am	
9am		9am		9am	
10am		10am		10am	
11am		11am		11am	
12pm		12pm		12pm	
1pm		1pm		1pm	
2pm		2pm		2pm	
3pm		3pm		3pm	
4pm		4pm		4pm	
5pm		5pm		5pm	
6pm		6pm		6pm	
7pm		7pm		7pm	
8pm		8pm		8pm	
9pm		9pm		9pm	
10pm		10pm		10pm	
11pm		11pm		11pm	
12pm		12pm		12pm	

Wheel of Life

To-do

Reflections

Notes

Quotations & Tips

POWERFUL
WOMEN
TODAY

| Month | | Year | |

SUNDAY ○	MONDAY ○	TUESDAY ○	WEDNESDAY ○
6am	6am	6am	6am
7am	7am	7am	7am
8am	8am	8am	8am
9am	9am	9am	9am
10am	10am	10am	10am
11am	11am	11am	11am
12pm	12pm	12pm	12pm
1pm	1pm	1pm	1pm
2pm	2pm	2pm	2pm
3pm	3pm	3pm	3pm
4pm	4pm	4pm	4pm
5pm	5pm	5pm	5pm
6pm	6pm	6pm	6pm
7pm	7pm	7pm	7pm
8pm	8pm	8pm	8pm
9pm	9pm	9pm	9pm
10pm	10pm	10pm	10pm
11pm	11pm	11pm	11pm
12pm	12pm	12pm	12pm

"Step out of the history that is holding you back. Step into the new story you are willing to create." – *Oprah Winfrey*

THURSDAY ⬤		FRIDAY ⬤		SATURDAY ⬤	
6am		6am		6am	
7am		7am		7am	
8am		8am		8am	
9am		9am		9am	
10am		10am		10am	
11am		11am		11am	
12pm		12pm		12pm	
1pm		1pm		1pm	
2pm		2pm		2pm	
3pm		3pm		3pm	
4pm		4pm		4pm	
5pm		5pm		5pm	
6pm		6pm		6pm	
7pm		7pm		7pm	
8pm		8pm		8pm	
9pm		9pm		9pm	
10pm		10pm		10pm	
11pm		11pm		11pm	
12pm		12pm		12pm	

Wheel of Life

To-do

Reflections

Notes

Quotations & Tips

POWERFUL WOMEN TODAY

| Month _____ | | Year _____ | |

SUNDAY ⚪	MONDAY ⚪	TUESDAY ⚪	WEDNESDAY ⚪
6am	6am	6am	6am
7am	7am	7am	7am
8am	8am	8am	8am
9am	9am	9am	9am
10am	10am	10am	10am
11am	11am	11am	11am
12pm	12pm	12pm	12pm
1pm	1pm	1pm	1pm
2pm	2pm	2pm	2pm
3pm	3pm	3pm	3pm
4pm	4pm	4pm	4pm
5pm	5pm	5pm	5pm
6pm	6pm	6pm	6pm
7pm	7pm	7pm	7pm
8pm	8pm	8pm	8pm
9pm	9pm	9pm	9pm
10pm	10pm	10pm	10pm
11pm	11pm	11pm	11pm
12pm	12pm	12pm	12pm

"What you do makes a difference, and you have to decide what kind of difference you want to make." – Jane Goodall

THURSDAY	⦿	FRIDAY	⦿	SATURDAY	⦿
6am		6am		6am	
7am		7am		7am	
8am		8am		8am	
9am		9am		9am	
10am		10am		10am	
11am		11am		11am	
12pm		12pm		12pm	
1pm		1pm		1pm	
2pm		2pm		2pm	
3pm		3pm		3pm	
4pm		4pm		4pm	
5pm		5pm		5pm	
6pm		6pm		6pm	
7pm		7pm		7pm	
8pm		8pm		8pm	
9pm		9pm		9pm	
10pm		10pm		10pm	
11pm		11pm		11pm	
12pm		12pm		12pm	

Wheel of Life

To-do

Reflections

Notes

Quotations & Tips

POWERFUL
WOMEN
TODAY

Month [   ] Year [   ]

SUNDAY ⬤	MONDAY ⬤	TUESDAY ⬤	WEDNESDAY ⬤
6am	6am	6am	6am
7am	7am	7am	7am
8am	8am	8am	8am
9am	9am	9am	9am
10am	10am	10am	10am
11am	11am	11am	11am
12pm	12pm	12pm	12pm
1pm	1pm	1pm	1pm
2pm	2pm	2pm	2pm
3pm	3pm	3pm	3pm
4pm	4pm	4pm	4pm
5pm	5pm	5pm	5pm
6pm	6pm	6pm	6pm
7pm	7pm	7pm	7pm
8pm	8pm	8pm	8pm
9pm	9pm	9pm	9pm
10pm	10pm	10pm	10pm
11pm	11pm	11pm	11pm
12pm	12pm	12pm	12pm

WEEKLY CHECK INS

THURSDAY ⦿		FRIDAY ⦿		SATURDAY ⦿	
6am		6am		6am	
7am		7am		7am	
8am		8am		8am	
9am		9am		9am	
10am		10am		10am	
11am		11am		11am	
12pm		12pm		12pm	
1pm		1pm		1pm	
2pm		2pm		2pm	
3pm		3pm		3pm	
4pm		4pm		4pm	
5pm		5pm		5pm	
6pm		6pm		6pm	
7pm		7pm		7pm	
8pm		8pm		8pm	
9pm		9pm		9pm	
10pm		10pm		10pm	
11pm		11pm		11pm	
12pm		12pm		12pm	

Wheel of Life

To-do

Reflections

Notes

Quotations & Tips

POWERFUL WOMEN TODAY

Month		Year	

SUNDAY ⬤	MONDAY ⬤	TUESDAY ⬤	WEDNESDAY ⬤
6am	6am	6am	6am
7am	7am	7am	7am
8am	8am	8am	8am
9am	9am	9am	9am
10am	10am	10am	10am
11am	11am	11am	11am
12pm	12pm	12pm	12pm
1pm	1pm	1pm	1pm
2pm	2pm	2pm	2pm
3pm	3pm	3pm	3pm
4pm	4pm	4pm	4pm
5pm	5pm	5pm	5pm
6pm	6pm	6pm	6pm
7pm	7pm	7pm	7pm
8pm	8pm	8pm	8pm
9pm	9pm	9pm	9pm
10pm	10pm	10pm	10pm
11pm	11pm	11pm	11pm
12pm	12pm	12pm	12pm

"A good compromise is one where everybody makes a contribution." – *Angela Merkel*

WEEKLY
CHECK INS

THURSDAY	⚪	FRIDAY	⚪	SATURDAY	⚪
6am		6am		6am	
7am		7am		7am	
8am		8am		8am	
9am		9am		9am	
10am		10am		10am	
11am		11am		11am	
12pm		12pm		12pm	
1pm		1pm		1pm	
2pm		2pm		2pm	
3pm		3pm		3pm	
4pm		4pm		4pm	
5pm		5pm		5pm	
6pm		6pm		6pm	
7pm		7pm		7pm	
8pm		8pm		8pm	
9pm		9pm		9pm	
10pm		10pm		10pm	
11pm		11pm		11pm	
12pm		12pm		12pm	

Wheel of Life

To-do

Reflections

Notes

Quotations & Tips

POWERFUL WOMEN TODAY

Month		Year	

SUNDAY ⬤	MONDAY ⬤	TUESDAY ⬤	WEDNESDAY ⬤
6am	6am	6am	6am
7am	7am	7am	7am
8am	8am	8am	8am
9am	9am	9am	9am
10am	10am	10am	10am
11am	11am	11am	11am
12pm	12pm	12pm	12pm
1pm	1pm	1pm	1pm
2pm	2pm	2pm	2pm
3pm	3pm	3pm	3pm
4pm	4pm	4pm	4pm
5pm	5pm	5pm	5pm
6pm	6pm	6pm	6pm
7pm	7pm	7pm	7pm
8pm	8pm	8pm	8pm
9pm	9pm	9pm	9pm
10pm	10pm	10pm	10pm
11pm	11pm	11pm	11pm
12pm	12pm	12pm	12pm

"A strong woman is a woman determined to do something others are determined not be done." – *Marge Piercy*

THURSDAY	⬤	FRIDAY	⬤	SATURDAY	⬤
6am		6am		6am	
7am		7am		7am	
8am		8am		8am	
9am		9am		9am	
10am		10am		10am	
11am		11am		11am	
12pm		12pm		12pm	
1pm		1pm		1pm	
2pm		2pm		2pm	
3pm		3pm		3pm	
4pm		4pm		4pm	
5pm		5pm		5pm	
6pm		6pm		6pm	
7pm		7pm		7pm	
8pm		8pm		8pm	
9pm		9pm		9pm	
10pm		10pm		10pm	
11pm		11pm		11pm	
12pm		12pm		12pm	

Wheel of Life

To-do

Reflections

Notes

Quotations & Tips

POWERFUL
WOMEN
TODAY

Month			Year	

SUNDAY	○	MONDAY	○	TUESDAY	○	WEDNESDAY	○
6am		6am		6am		6am	
7am		7am		7am		7am	
8am		8am		8am		8am	
9am		9am		9am		9am	
10am		10am		10am		10am	
11am		11am		11am		11am	
12pm		12pm		12pm		12pm	
1pm		1pm		1pm		1pm	
2pm		2pm		2pm		2pm	
3pm		3pm		3pm		3pm	
4pm		4pm		4pm		4pm	
5pm		5pm		5pm		5pm	
6pm		6pm		6pm		6pm	
7pm		7pm		7pm		7pm	
8pm		8pm		8pm		8pm	
9pm		9pm		9pm		9pm	
10pm		10pm		10pm		10pm	
11pm		11pm		11pm		11pm	
12pm		12pm		12pm		12pm	

"I choose to make the rest of my life the best of my life."
— Louise Hay

WEEKLY
CHECK INS

THURSDAY ⬤		FRIDAY ⬤		SATURDAY ⬤	
6am		6am		6am	
7am		7am		7am	
8am		8am		8am	
9am		9am		9am	
10am		10am		10am	
11am		11am		11am	
12pm		12pm		12pm	
1pm		1pm		1pm	
2pm		2pm		2pm	
3pm		3pm		3pm	
4pm		4pm		4pm	
5pm		5pm		5pm	
6pm		6pm		6pm	
7pm		7pm		7pm	
8pm		8pm		8pm	
9pm		9pm		9pm	
10pm		10pm		10pm	
11pm		11pm		11pm	
12pm		12pm		12pm	

Wheel of Life

To-do

Reflections

Notes

Quotations & Tips

POWERFUL
WOMEN TODAY

Month		Year	

SUNDAY ●	MONDAY ●	TUESDAY ●	WEDNESDAY ●
6am	6am	6am	6am
7am	7am	7am	7am
8am	8am	8am	8am
9am	9am	9am	9am
10am	10am	10am	10am
11am	11am	11am	11am
12pm	12pm	12pm	12pm
1pm	1pm	1pm	1pm
2pm	2pm	2pm	2pm
3pm	3pm	3pm	3pm
4pm	4pm	4pm	4pm
5pm	5pm	5pm	5pm
6pm	6pm	6pm	6pm
7pm	7pm	7pm	7pm
8pm	8pm	8pm	8pm
9pm	9pm	9pm	9pm
10pm	10pm	10pm	10pm
11pm	11pm	11pm	11pm
12pm	12pm	12pm	12pm

"Drama is very important in life: You have to come on with a bang. You never want to go out with a whimper." — *Julia Child*

WEEKLY
CHECK INS

THURSDAY	○	FRIDAY	○	SATURDAY	○
6am		6am		6am	
7am		7am		7am	
8am		8am		8am	
9am		9am		9am	
10am		10am		10am	
11am		11am		11am	
12pm		12pm		12pm	
1pm		1pm		1pm	
2pm		2pm		2pm	
3pm		3pm		3pm	
4pm		4pm		4pm	
5pm		5pm		5pm	
6pm		6pm		6pm	
7pm		7pm		7pm	
8pm		8pm		8pm	
9pm		9pm		9pm	
10pm		10pm		10pm	
11pm		11pm		11pm	
12pm		12pm		12pm	

Wheel of Life

To-do

Reflections

Notes

Quotations & Tips

POWERFUL
WOMEN TODAY

Month [   ]   Year [   ]

SUNDAY ⬤		MONDAY ⬤		TUESDAY ⬤		WEDNESDAY ⬤	
6am		6am		6am		6am	
7am		7am		7am		7am	
8am		8am		8am		8am	
9am		9am		9am		9am	
10am		10am		10am		10am	
11am		11am		11am		11am	
12pm		12pm		12pm		12pm	
1pm		1pm		1pm		1pm	
2pm		2pm		2pm		2pm	
3pm		3pm		3pm		3pm	
4pm		4pm		4pm		4pm	
5pm		5pm		5pm		5pm	
6pm		6pm		6pm		6pm	
7pm		7pm		7pm		7pm	
8pm		8pm		8pm		8pm	
9pm		9pm		9pm		9pm	
10pm		10pm		10pm		10pm	
11pm		11pm		11pm		11pm	
12pm		12pm		12pm		12pm	

THURSDAY	○	FRIDAY	○	SATURDAY	○
6am		6am		6am	
7am		7am		7am	
8am		8am		8am	
9am		9am		9am	
10am		10am		10am	
11am		11am		11am	
12pm		12pm		12pm	
1pm		1pm		1pm	
2pm		2pm		2pm	
3pm		3pm		3pm	
4pm		4pm		4pm	
5pm		5pm		5pm	
6pm		6pm		6pm	
7pm		7pm		7pm	
8pm		8pm		8pm	
9pm		9pm		9pm	
10pm		10pm		10pm	
11pm		11pm		11pm	
12pm		12pm		12pm	

WEEKLY
CHECK INS

Wheel of Life

To-do

Reflections

Notes

Quotations & Tips

POWERFUL
WOMEN
TODAY

Month		Year	

SUNDAY ⬤	MONDAY ⬤	TUESDAY ⬤	WEDNESDAY ⬤
6am	6am	6am	6am
7am	7am	7am	7am
8am	8am	8am	8am
9am	9am	9am	9am
10am	10am	10am	10am
11am	11am	11am	11am
12pm	12pm	12pm	12pm
1pm	1pm	1pm	1pm
2pm	2pm	2pm	2pm
3pm	3pm	3pm	3pm
4pm	4pm	4pm	4pm
5pm	5pm	5pm	5pm
6pm	6pm	6pm	6pm
7pm	7pm	7pm	7pm
8pm	8pm	8pm	8pm
9pm	9pm	9pm	9pm
10pm	10pm	10pm	10pm
11pm	11pm	11pm	11pm
12pm	12pm	12pm	12pm

"The question isn't who is going to let me: it's who is going to stop me." – *Ayn Rand*

THURSDAY ○		FRIDAY ○		SATURDAY ○	
6am		6am		6am	
7am		7am		7am	
8am		8am		8am	
9am		9am		9am	
10am		10am		10am	
11am		11am		11am	
12pm		12pm		12pm	
1pm		1pm		1pm	
2pm		2pm		2pm	
3pm		3pm		3pm	
4pm		4pm		4pm	
5pm		5pm		5pm	
6pm		6pm		6pm	
7pm		7pm		7pm	
8pm		8pm		8pm	
9pm		9pm		9pm	
10pm		10pm		10pm	
11pm		11pm		11pm	
12pm		12pm		12pm	

Wheel of Life

To-do

Reflections

Notes

Quotations & Tips

POWERFUL WOMEN TODAY

Month [   ] Year [   ]

SUNDAY ●	MONDAY ●	TUESDAY ●	WEDNESDAY ●
6am	6am	6am	6am
7am	7am	7am	7am
8am	8am	8am	8am
9am	9am	9am	9am
10am	10am	10am	10am
11am	11am	11am	11am
12pm	12pm	12pm	12pm
1pm	1pm	1pm	1pm
2pm	2pm	2pm	2pm
3pm	3pm	3pm	3pm
4pm	4pm	4pm	4pm
5pm	5pm	5pm	5pm
6pm	6pm	6pm	6pm
7pm	7pm	7pm	7pm
8pm	8pm	8pm	8pm
9pm	9pm	9pm	9pm
10pm	10pm	10pm	10pm
11pm	11pm	11pm	11pm
12pm	12pm	12pm	12pm

> *"Women will only have true equality when men share with them the responsibility of bringing up the next generation."*
> *— Ruth Bader Ginsberg*

THURSDAY		FRIDAY		SATURDAY	
6am		6am		6am	
7am		7am		7am	
8am		8am		8am	
9am		9am		9am	
10am		10am		10am	
11am		11am		11am	
12pm		12pm		12pm	
1pm		1pm		1pm	
2pm		2pm		2pm	
3pm		3pm		3pm	
4pm		4pm		4pm	
5pm		5pm		5pm	
6pm		6pm		6pm	
7pm		7pm		7pm	
8pm		8pm		8pm	
9pm		9pm		9pm	
10pm		10pm		10pm	
11pm		11pm		11pm	
12pm		12pm		12pm	

WEEKLY
CHECK INS

Wheel of Life

To-do

Reflections

Notes

Quotations & Tips

POWERFUL WOMEN TODAY

Month [ ] Year [ ]

SUNDAY ●		MONDAY ●		TUESDAY ●		WEDNESDAY ●	
6am		6am		6am		6am	
7am		7am		7am		7am	
8am		8am		8am		8am	
9am		9am		9am		9am	
10am		10am		10am		10am	
11am		11am		11am		11am	
12pm		12pm		12pm		12pm	
1pm		1pm		1pm		1pm	
2pm		2pm		2pm		2pm	
3pm		3pm		3pm		3pm	
4pm		4pm		4pm		4pm	
5pm		5pm		5pm		5pm	
6pm		6pm		6pm		6pm	
7pm		7pm		7pm		7pm	
8pm		8pm		8pm		8pm	
9pm		9pm		9pm		9pm	
10pm		10pm		10pm		10pm	
11pm		11pm		11pm		11pm	
12pm		12pm		12pm		12pm	

WEEKLY
CHECK INS

THURSDAY ○		FRIDAY ○		SATURDAY ○	
6am		6am		6am	
7am		7am		7am	
8am		8am		8am	
9am		9am		9am	
10am		10am		10am	
11am		11am		11am	
12pm		12pm		12pm	
1pm		1pm		1pm	
2pm		2pm		2pm	
3pm		3pm		3pm	
4pm		4pm		4pm	
5pm		5pm		5pm	
6pm		6pm		6pm	
7pm		7pm		7pm	
8pm		8pm		8pm	
9pm		9pm		9pm	
10pm		10pm		10pm	
11pm		11pm		11pm	
12pm		12pm		12pm	

Wheel of Life

To-do

Reflections

Notes

Quotations & Tips

POWERFUL
WOMEN TODAY

Month		Year	

SUNDAY	●	MONDAY	●	TUESDAY	●	WEDNESDAY	●
6am		6am		6am		6am	
7am		7am		7am		7am	
8am		8am		8am		8am	
9am		9am		9am		9am	
10am		10am		10am		10am	
11am		11am		11am		11am	
12pm		12pm		12pm		12pm	
1pm		1pm		1pm		1pm	
2pm		2pm		2pm		2pm	
3pm		3pm		3pm		3pm	
4pm		4pm		4pm		4pm	
5pm		5pm		5pm		5pm	
6pm		6pm		6pm		6pm	
7pm		7pm		7pm		7pm	
8pm		8pm		8pm		8pm	
9pm		9pm		9pm		9pm	
10pm		10pm		10pm		10pm	
11pm		11pm		11pm		11pm	
12pm		12pm		12pm		12pm	

"It's one of the greatest gifts you can give yourself, to forgive. Forgive everybody." — *Maya Angelou*

THURSDAY ⬤		FRIDAY ⬤		SATURDAY ⬤	
6am		6am		6am	
7am		7am		7am	
8am		8am		8am	
9am		9am		9am	
10am		10am		10am	
11am		11am		11am	
12pm		12pm		12pm	
1pm		1pm		1pm	
2pm		2pm		2pm	
3pm		3pm		3pm	
4pm		4pm		4pm	
5pm		5pm		5pm	
6pm		6pm		6pm	
7pm		7pm		7pm	
8pm		8pm		8pm	
9pm		9pm		9pm	
10pm		10pm		10pm	
11pm		11pm		11pm	
12pm		12pm		12pm	

Wheel of Life

To-do

Reflections

Notes

Quotations & Tips

POWERFUL
WOMEN
TODAY

Month		Year	

SUNDAY ⬤	MONDAY ⬤	TUESDAY ⬤	WEDNESDAY ⬤
6am	6am	6am	6am
7am	7am	7am	7am
8am	8am	8am	8am
9am	9am	9am	9am
10am	10am	10am	10am
11am	11am	11am	11am
12pm	12pm	12pm	12pm
1pm	1pm	1pm	1pm
2pm	2pm	2pm	2pm
3pm	3pm	3pm	3pm
4pm	4pm	4pm	4pm
5pm	5pm	5pm	5pm
6pm	6pm	6pm	6pm
7pm	7pm	7pm	7pm
8pm	8pm	8pm	8pm
9pm	9pm	9pm	9pm
10pm	10pm	10pm	10pm
11pm	11pm	11pm	11pm
12pm	12pm	12pm	12pm

WEEKLY
CHECK INS

THURSDAY	●	FRIDAY	●	SATURDAY	●
6am		6am		6am	
7am		7am		7am	
8am		8am		8am	
9am		9am		9am	
10am		10am		10am	
11am		11am		11am	
12pm		12pm		12pm	
1pm		1pm		1pm	
2pm		2pm		2pm	
3pm		3pm		3pm	
4pm		4pm		4pm	
5pm		5pm		5pm	
6pm		6pm		6pm	
7pm		7pm		7pm	
8pm		8pm		8pm	
9pm		9pm		9pm	
10pm		10pm		10pm	
11pm		11pm		11pm	
12pm		12pm		12pm	

Wheel of Life

To-do

Reflections

Notes

Quotations & Tips

POWERFUL
WOMEN TODAY

Month [   ] Year [   ]

SUNDAY ○	MONDAY ○	TUESDAY ○	WEDNESDAY ○
6am	6am	6am	6am
7am	7am	7am	7am
8am	8am	8am	8am
9am	9am	9am	9am
10am	10am	10am	10am
11am	11am	11am	11am
12pm	12pm	12pm	12pm
1pm	1pm	1pm	1pm
2pm	2pm	2pm	2pm
3pm	3pm	3pm	3pm
4pm	4pm	4pm	4pm
5pm	5pm	5pm	5pm
6pm	6pm	6pm	6pm
7pm	7pm	7pm	7pm
8pm	8pm	8pm	8pm
9pm	9pm	9pm	9pm
10pm	10pm	10pm	10pm
11pm	11pm	11pm	11pm
12pm	12pm	12pm	12pm

"A surplus of effort could overcome a deficit of confidence." – *Sonia Sotomayor*

THURSDAY		FRIDAY		SATURDAY	
6am		6am		6am	
7am		7am		7am	
8am		8am		8am	
9am		9am		9am	
10am		10am		10am	
11am		11am		11am	
12pm		12pm		12pm	
1pm		1pm		1pm	
2pm		2pm		2pm	
3pm		3pm		3pm	
4pm		4pm		4pm	
5pm		5pm		5pm	
6pm		6pm		6pm	
7pm		7pm		7pm	
8pm		8pm		8pm	
9pm		9pm		9pm	
10pm		10pm		10pm	
11pm		11pm		11pm	
12pm		12pm		12pm	

Wheel of Life

To-do

Reflections

Notes

Quotations & Tips

POWERFUL WOMEN TODAY

Month		Year	

SUNDAY ⬤		MONDAY ⬤		TUESDAY ⬤		WEDNESDAY ⬤	
6am		6am		6am		6am	
7am		7am		7am		7am	
8am		8am		8am		8am	
9am		9am		9am		9am	
10am		10am		10am		10am	
11am		11am		11am		11am	
12pm		12pm		12pm		12pm	
1pm		1pm		1pm		1pm	
2pm		2pm		2pm		2pm	
3pm		3pm		3pm		3pm	
4pm		4pm		4pm		4pm	
5pm		5pm		5pm		5pm	
6pm		6pm		6pm		6pm	
7pm		7pm		7pm		7pm	
8pm		8pm		8pm		8pm	
9pm		9pm		9pm		9pm	
10pm		10pm		10pm		10pm	
11pm		11pm		11pm		11pm	
12pm		12pm		12pm		12pm	

WEEKLY CHECK INS

THURSDAY	○	FRIDAY	○	SATURDAY	○
6am		6am		6am	
7am		7am		7am	
8am		8am		8am	
9am		9am		9am	
10am		10am		10am	
11am		11am		11am	
12pm		12pm		12pm	
1pm		1pm		1pm	
2pm		2pm		2pm	
3pm		3pm		3pm	
4pm		4pm		4pm	
5pm		5pm		5pm	
6pm		6pm		6pm	
7pm		7pm		7pm	
8pm		8pm		8pm	
9pm		9pm		9pm	
10pm		10pm		10pm	
11pm		11pm		11pm	
12pm		12pm		12pm	

Wheel of Life

To-do

Reflections

Notes

Quotations & Tips

POWERFUL WOMEN TODAY

Month | Year

SUNDAY ●	MONDAY ●	TUESDAY ●	WEDNESDAY ●
6am	6am	6am	6am
7am	7am	7am	7am
8am	8am	8am	8am
9am	9am	9am	9am
10am	10am	10am	10am
11am	11am	11am	11am
12pm	12pm	12pm	12pm
1pm	1pm	1pm	1pm
2pm	2pm	2pm	2pm
3pm	3pm	3pm	3pm
4pm	4pm	4pm	4pm
5pm	5pm	5pm	5pm
6pm	6pm	6pm	6pm
7pm	7pm	7pm	7pm
8pm	8pm	8pm	8pm
9pm	9pm	9pm	9pm
10pm	10pm	10pm	10pm
11pm	11pm	11pm	11pm
12pm	12pm	12pm	12pm

WEEKLY
CHECK INS

THURSDAY	⬤	FRIDAY	⬤	SATURDAY	⬤
6am		6am		6am	
7am		7am		7am	
8am		8am		8am	
9am		9am		9am	
10am		10am		10am	
11am		11am		11am	
12pm		12pm		12pm	
1pm		1pm		1pm	
2pm		2pm		2pm	
3pm		3pm		3pm	
4pm		4pm		4pm	
5pm		5pm		5pm	
6pm		6pm		6pm	
7pm		7pm		7pm	
8pm		8pm		8pm	
9pm		9pm		9pm	
10pm		10pm		10pm	
11pm		11pm		11pm	
12pm		12pm		12pm	

Wheel of Life

To-do

Reflections

Notes

Quotations & Tips

POWERFUL
WOMEN TODAY

Month		Year	

SUNDAY ⬤	MONDAY ⬤	TUESDAY ⬤	WEDNESDAY ⬤
6am	6am	6am	6am
7am	7am	7am	7am
8am	8am	8am	8am
9am	9am	9am	9am
10am	10am	10am	10am
11am	11am	11am	11am
12pm	12pm	12pm	12pm
1pm	1pm	1pm	1pm
2pm	2pm	2pm	2pm
3pm	3pm	3pm	3pm
4pm	4pm	4pm	4pm
5pm	5pm	5pm	5pm
6pm	6pm	6pm	6pm
7pm	7pm	7pm	7pm
8pm	8pm	8pm	8pm
9pm	9pm	9pm	9pm
10pm	10pm	10pm	10pm
11pm	11pm	11pm	11pm
12pm	12pm	12pm	12pm

"Hold your head and your standards high even as people or circumstances try to pull you down." — *Tory Johnson*

THURSDAY	⬤	FRIDAY	⬤	SATURDAY	⬤
6am		6am		6am	
7am		7am		7am	
8am		8am		8am	
9am		9am		9am	
10am		10am		10am	
11am		11am		11am	
12pm		12pm		12pm	
1pm		1pm		1pm	
2pm		2pm		2pm	
3pm		3pm		3pm	
4pm		4pm		4pm	
5pm		5pm		5pm	
6pm		6pm		6pm	
7pm		7pm		7pm	
8pm		8pm		8pm	
9pm		9pm		9pm	
10pm		10pm		10pm	
11pm		11pm		11pm	
12pm		12pm		12pm	

Wheel of Life

To-do

Reflections

Notes

Quotations & Tips

POWERFUL WOMEN TODAY

Month		Year	

SUNDAY	●	MONDAY	●	TUESDAY	●	WEDNESDAY	●
6am		6am		6am		6am	
7am		7am		7am		7am	
8am		8am		8am		8am	
9am		9am		9am		9am	
10am		10am		10am		10am	
11am		11am		11am		11am	
12pm		12pm		12pm		12pm	
1pm		1pm		1pm		1pm	
2pm		2pm		2pm		2pm	
3pm		3pm		3pm		3pm	
4pm		4pm		4pm		4pm	
5pm		5pm		5pm		5pm	
6pm		6pm		6pm		6pm	
7pm		7pm		7pm		7pm	
8pm		8pm		8pm		8pm	
9pm		9pm		9pm		9pm	
10pm		10pm		10pm		10pm	
11pm		11pm		11pm		11pm	
12pm		12pm		12pm		12pm	

"The best thing to hold onto in life is each other."
— Audrey Hepburn

THURSDAY ⚪		FRIDAY ⚪		SATURDAY ⚪	
6am		6am		6am	
7am		7am		7am	
8am		8am		8am	
9am		9am		9am	
10am		10am		10am	
11am		11am		11am	
12pm		12pm		12pm	
1pm		1pm		1pm	
2pm		2pm		2pm	
3pm		3pm		3pm	
4pm		4pm		4pm	
5pm		5pm		5pm	
6pm		6pm		6pm	
7pm		7pm		7pm	
8pm		8pm		8pm	
9pm		9pm		9pm	
10pm		10pm		10pm	
11pm		11pm		11pm	
12pm		12pm		12pm	

Wheel of Life

To-do

Reflections

Notes

Quotations & Tips

POWERFUL WOMEN TODAY

Month			Year	

SUNDAY ⬤	MONDAY ⬤	TUESDAY ⬤	WEDNESDAY ⬤
6am	6am	6am	6am
7am	7am	7am	7am
8am	8am	8am	8am
9am	9am	9am	9am
10am	10am	10am	10am
11am	11am	11am	11am
12pm	12pm	12pm	12pm
1pm	1pm	1pm	1pm
2pm	2pm	2pm	2pm
3pm	3pm	3pm	3pm
4pm	4pm	4pm	4pm
5pm	5pm	5pm	5pm
6pm	6pm	6pm	6pm
7pm	7pm	7pm	7pm
8pm	8pm	8pm	8pm
9pm	9pm	9pm	9pm
10pm	10pm	10pm	10pm
11pm	11pm	11pm	11pm
12pm	12pm	12pm	12pm

"Normal is not something to aspire to, it's something to get away from." – Jodie Foster

THURSDAY		FRIDAY		SATURDAY	
6am		6am		6am	
7am		7am		7am	
8am		8am		8am	
9am		9am		9am	
10am		10am		10am	
11am		11am		11am	
12pm		12pm		12pm	
1pm		1pm		1pm	
2pm		2pm		2pm	
3pm		3pm		3pm	
4pm		4pm		4pm	
5pm		5pm		5pm	
6pm		6pm		6pm	
7pm		7pm		7pm	
8pm		8pm		8pm	
9pm		9pm		9pm	
10pm		10pm		10pm	
11pm		11pm		11pm	
12pm		12pm		12pm	

Wheel of Life

To-do

Reflections

Notes

Quotations & Tips

POWERFUL
WOMEN
TODAY

Month			Year	

SUNDAY	●	MONDAY	●	TUESDAY	●	WEDNESDAY	●
6am		6am		6am		6am	
7am		7am		7am		7am	
8am		8am		8am		8am	
9am		9am		9am		9am	
10am		10am		10am		10am	
11am		11am		11am		11am	
12pm		12pm		12pm		12pm	
1pm		1pm		1pm		1pm	
2pm		2pm		2pm		2pm	
3pm		3pm		3pm		3pm	
4pm		4pm		4pm		4pm	
5pm		5pm		5pm		5pm	
6pm		6pm		6pm		6pm	
7pm		7pm		7pm		7pm	
8pm		8pm		8pm		8pm	
9pm		9pm		9pm		9pm	
10pm		10pm		10pm		10pm	
11pm		11pm		11pm		11pm	
12pm		12pm		12pm		12pm	

"Owning our story can be hard but not nearly as difficult as spending our lives running from it." — *Brene Brown*

THURSDAY ⬤	FRIDAY ⬤	SATURDAY ⬤
6am	6am	6am
7am	7am	7am
8am	8am	8am
9am	9am	9am
10am	10am	10am
11am	11am	11am
12pm	12pm	12pm
1pm	1pm	1pm
2pm	2pm	2pm
3pm	3pm	3pm
4pm	4pm	4pm
5pm	5pm	5pm
6pm	6pm	6pm
7pm	7pm	7pm
8pm	8pm	8pm
9pm	9pm	9pm
10pm	10pm	10pm
11pm	11pm	11pm
12pm	12pm	12pm

Wheel of Life

To-do

Reflections

Notes

Quotations & Tips

POWERFUL WOMEN TODAY

Month   Year

SUNDAY ●		MONDAY ●		TUESDAY ●		WEDNESDAY ●	
6am		6am		6am		6am	
7am		7am		7am		7am	
8am		8am		8am		8am	
9am		9am		9am		9am	
10am		10am		10am		10am	
11am		11am		11am		11am	
12pm		12pm		12pm		12pm	
1pm		1pm		1pm		1pm	
2pm		2pm		2pm		2pm	
3pm		3pm		3pm		3pm	
4pm		4pm		4pm		4pm	
5pm		5pm		5pm		5pm	
6pm		6pm		6pm		6pm	
7pm		7pm		7pm		7pm	
8pm		8pm		8pm		8pm	
9pm		9pm		9pm		9pm	
10pm		10pm		10pm		10pm	
11pm		11pm		11pm		11pm	
12pm		12pm		12pm		12pm	

"I do not try to dance better than anyone else. I only try to dance better than myself." — *Arianna Huffington*

THURSDAY	⬤	FRIDAY	⬤	SATURDAY	⬤
6am		6am		6am	
7am		7am		7am	
8am		8am		8am	
9am		9am		9am	
10am		10am		10am	
11am		11am		11am	
12pm		12pm		12pm	
1pm		1pm		1pm	
2pm		2pm		2pm	
3pm		3pm		3pm	
4pm		4pm		4pm	
5pm		5pm		5pm	
6pm		6pm		6pm	
7pm		7pm		7pm	
8pm		8pm		8pm	
9pm		9pm		9pm	
10pm		10pm		10pm	
11pm		11pm		11pm	
12pm		12pm		12pm	

WEEKLY
CHECK INS

Wheel of Life

To-do

Reflections

Notes

Quotations & Tips

POWERFUL
WOMEN TODAY

Month		Year	

SUNDAY ⚪	MONDAY ⚪	TUESDAY ⚪	WEDNESDAY ⚪
6am	6am	6am	6am
7am	7am	7am	7am
8am	8am	8am	8am
9am	9am	9am	9am
10am	10am	10am	10am
11am	11am	11am	11am
12pm	12pm	12pm	12pm
1pm	1pm	1pm	1pm
2pm	2pm	2pm	2pm
3pm	3pm	3pm	3pm
4pm	4pm	4pm	4pm
5pm	5pm	5pm	5pm
6pm	6pm	6pm	6pm
7pm	7pm	7pm	7pm
8pm	8pm	8pm	8pm
9pm	9pm	9pm	9pm
10pm	10pm	10pm	10pm
11pm	11pm	11pm	11pm
12pm	12pm	12pm	12pm

"Everyone shines, given the right lighting." — *Susan Cain*

THURSDAY	⭕	FRIDAY	⭕	SATURDAY	⭕
6am		6am		6am	
7am		7am		7am	
8am		8am		8am	
9am		9am		9am	
10am		10am		10am	
11am		11am		11am	
12pm		12pm		12pm	
1pm		1pm		1pm	
2pm		2pm		2pm	
3pm		3pm		3pm	
4pm		4pm		4pm	
5pm		5pm		5pm	
6pm		6pm		6pm	
7pm		7pm		7pm	
8pm		8pm		8pm	
9pm		9pm		9pm	
10pm		10pm		10pm	
11pm		11pm		11pm	
12pm		12pm		12pm	

Wheel of Life

To-do

Reflections

Notes

Quotations & Tips

POWERFUL
WOMEN TODAY

Month [   ] Year [   ]

SUNDAY ●		MONDAY ●		TUESDAY ●		WEDNESDAY ●	
6am		6am		6am		6am	
7am		7am		7am		7am	
8am		8am		8am		8am	
9am		9am		9am		9am	
10am		10am		10am		10am	
11am		11am		11am		11am	
12pm		12pm		12pm		12pm	
1pm		1pm		1pm		1pm	
2pm		2pm		2pm		2pm	
3pm		3pm		3pm		3pm	
4pm		4pm		4pm		4pm	
5pm		5pm		5pm		5pm	
6pm		6pm		6pm		6pm	
7pm		7pm		7pm		7pm	
8pm		8pm		8pm		8pm	
9pm		9pm		9pm		9pm	
10pm		10pm		10pm		10pm	
11pm		11pm		11pm		11pm	
12pm		12pm		12pm		12pm	

"You can't be that kid standing at the top of the waterslide, overthinking it. You have to go down the chute."

— Tina Fey

THURSDAY ⬤		FRIDAY ⬤		SATURDAY ⬤	
6am		6am		6am	
7am		7am		7am	
8am		8am		8am	
9am		9am		9am	
10am		10am		10am	
11am		11am		11am	
12pm		12pm		12pm	
1pm		1pm		1pm	
2pm		2pm		2pm	
3pm		3pm		3pm	
4pm		4pm		4pm	
5pm		5pm		5pm	
6pm		6pm		6pm	
7pm		7pm		7pm	
8pm		8pm		8pm	
9pm		9pm		9pm	
10pm		10pm		10pm	
11pm		11pm		11pm	
12pm		12pm		12pm	

WEEKLY
CHECK INS

Wheel of Life

To-do

Reflections

Notes

Quotations & Tips

POWERFUL WOMEN TODAY

Month [   ] Year [   ]

SUNDAY ⬤	MONDAY ⬤	TUESDAY ⬤	WEDNESDAY ⬤
6am	6am	6am	6am
7am	7am	7am	7am
8am	8am	8am	8am
9am	9am	9am	9am
10am	10am	10am	10am
11am	11am	11am	11am
12pm	12pm	12pm	12pm
1pm	1pm	1pm	1pm
2pm	2pm	2pm	2pm
3pm	3pm	3pm	3pm
4pm	4pm	4pm	4pm
5pm	5pm	5pm	5pm
6pm	6pm	6pm	6pm
7pm	7pm	7pm	7pm
8pm	8pm	8pm	8pm
9pm	9pm	9pm	9pm
10pm	10pm	10pm	10pm
11pm	11pm	11pm	11pm
12pm	12pm	12pm	12pm

"The challenge is not to be perfect...it's to be whole."
— *Jane Fonda*

WEEKLY CHECK INS

THURSDAY ⭕		FRIDAY ⭕		SATURDAY ⭕	
6am		6am		6am	
7am		7am		7am	
8am		8am		8am	
9am		9am		9am	
10am		10am		10am	
11am		11am		11am	
12pm		12pm		12pm	
1pm		1pm		1pm	
2pm		2pm		2pm	
3pm		3pm		3pm	
4pm		4pm		4pm	
5pm		5pm		5pm	
6pm		6pm		6pm	
7pm		7pm		7pm	
8pm		8pm		8pm	
9pm		9pm		9pm	
10pm		10pm		10pm	
11pm		11pm		11pm	
12pm		12pm		12pm	

Wheel of Life

To-do

Reflections

Notes

Quotations & Tips

POWERFUL WOMEN TODAY

Month [   ] Year [   ]

SUNDAY ⬤		MONDAY ⬤		TUESDAY ⬤		WEDNESDAY ⬤	
6am		6am		6am		6am	
7am		7am		7am		7am	
8am		8am		8am		8am	
9am		9am		9am		9am	
10am		10am		10am		10am	
11am		11am		11am		11am	
12pm		12pm		12pm		12pm	
1pm		1pm		1pm		1pm	
2pm		2pm		2pm		2pm	
3pm		3pm		3pm		3pm	
4pm		4pm		4pm		4pm	
5pm		5pm		5pm		5pm	
6pm		6pm		6pm		6pm	
7pm		7pm		7pm		7pm	
8pm		8pm		8pm		8pm	
9pm		9pm		9pm		9pm	
10pm		10pm		10pm		10pm	
11pm		11pm		11pm		11pm	
12pm		12pm		12pm		12pm	

"You have trust in what you think. If you splinter yourself and try to please everyone, you can't." – Annie Lebovitz

WEEKLY
CHECK INS

THURSDAY	○	FRIDAY	○	SATURDAY	○
6am		6am		6am	
7am		7am		7am	
8am		8am		8am	
9am		9am		9am	
10am		10am		10am	
11am		11am		11am	
12pm		12pm		12pm	
1pm		1pm		1pm	
2pm		2pm		2pm	
3pm		3pm		3pm	
4pm		4pm		4pm	
5pm		5pm		5pm	
6pm		6pm		6pm	
7pm		7pm		7pm	
8pm		8pm		8pm	
9pm		9pm		9pm	
10pm		10pm		10pm	
11pm		11pm		11pm	
12pm		12pm		12pm	

Wheel of Life

To-do

Reflections

Notes

Quotations & Tips

POWERFUL
WOMEN TODAY

Month

Year

SUNDAY	●	MONDAY	●	TUESDAY	●	WEDNESDAY	●
6am		6am		6am		6am	
7am		7am		7am		7am	
8am		8am		8am		8am	
9am		9am		9am		9am	
10am		10am		10am		10am	
11am		11am		11am		11am	
12pm		12pm		12pm		12pm	
1pm		1pm		1pm		1pm	
2pm		2pm		2pm		2pm	
3pm		3pm		3pm		3pm	
4pm		4pm		4pm		4pm	
5pm		5pm		5pm		5pm	
6pm		6pm		6pm		6pm	
7pm		7pm		7pm		7pm	
8pm		8pm		8pm		8pm	
9pm		9pm		9pm		9pm	
10pm		10pm		10pm		10pm	
11pm		11pm		11pm		11pm	
12pm		12pm		12pm		12pm	

WEEKLY
CHECK INS

THURSDAY	⬤	FRIDAY	⬤	SATURDAY	⬤
6am		6am		6am	
7am		7am		7am	
8am		8am		8am	
9am		9am		9am	
10am		10am		10am	
11am		11am		11am	
12pm		12pm		12pm	
1pm		1pm		1pm	
2pm		2pm		2pm	
3pm		3pm		3pm	
4pm		4pm		4pm	
5pm		5pm		5pm	
6pm		6pm		6pm	
7pm		7pm		7pm	
8pm		8pm		8pm	
9pm		9pm		9pm	
10pm		10pm		10pm	
11pm		11pm		11pm	
12pm		12pm		12pm	

Wheel of Life

To-do

Reflections

Notes

Quotations & Tips

POWERFUL WOMEN TODAY

Month		Year	

SUNDAY ●	MONDAY ●	TUESDAY ●	WEDNESDAY ●
6am	6am	6am	6am
7am	7am	7am	7am
8am	8am	8am	8am
9am	9am	9am	9am
10am	10am	10am	10am
11am	11am	11am	11am
12pm	12pm	12pm	12pm
1pm	1pm	1pm	1pm
2pm	2pm	2pm	2pm
3pm	3pm	3pm	3pm
4pm	4pm	4pm	4pm
5pm	5pm	5pm	5pm
6pm	6pm	6pm	6pm
7pm	7pm	7pm	7pm
8pm	8pm	8pm	8pm
9pm	9pm	9pm	9pm
10pm	10pm	10pm	10pm
11pm	11pm	11pm	11pm
12pm	12pm	12pm	12pm

WEEKLY
CHECK INS

THURSDAY	⬤	FRIDAY	⬤	SATURDAY	⬤
6am		6am		6am	
7am		7am		7am	
8am		8am		8am	
9am		9am		9am	
10am		10am		10am	
11am		11am		11am	
12pm		12pm		12pm	
1pm		1pm		1pm	
2pm		2pm		2pm	
3pm		3pm		3pm	
4pm		4pm		4pm	
5pm		5pm		5pm	
6pm		6pm		6pm	
7pm		7pm		7pm	
8pm		8pm		8pm	
9pm		9pm		9pm	
10pm		10pm		10pm	
11pm		11pm		11pm	
12pm		12pm		12pm	

Wheel of Life

To-do

Reflections

Notes

Quotations & Tips

POWERFUL WOMEN TODAY

Month [   ] Year [   ]

SUNDAY ⚪		MONDAY ⚪		TUESDAY ⚪		WEDNESDAY ⚪	
6am		6am		6am		6am	
7am		7am		7am		7am	
8am		8am		8am		8am	
9am		9am		9am		9am	
10am		10am		10am		10am	
11am		11am		11am		11am	
12pm		12pm		12pm		12pm	
1pm		1pm		1pm		1pm	
2pm		2pm		2pm		2pm	
3pm		3pm		3pm		3pm	
4pm		4pm		4pm		4pm	
5pm		5pm		5pm		5pm	
6pm		6pm		6pm		6pm	
7pm		7pm		7pm		7pm	
8pm		8pm		8pm		8pm	
9pm		9pm		9pm		9pm	
10pm		10pm		10pm		10pm	
11pm		11pm		11pm		11pm	
12pm		12pm		12pm		12pm	

"Dying seems less sad than having lived too little."
– Gloria Steinem

THURSDAY	⚪	FRIDAY	⚪	SATURDAY	⚪
6am		6am		6am	
7am		7am		7am	
8am		8am		8am	
9am		9am		9am	
10am		10am		10am	
11am		11am		11am	
12pm		12pm		12pm	
1pm		1pm		1pm	
2pm		2pm		2pm	
3pm		3pm		3pm	
4pm		4pm		4pm	
5pm		5pm		5pm	
6pm		6pm		6pm	
7pm		7pm		7pm	
8pm		8pm		8pm	
9pm		9pm		9pm	
10pm		10pm		10pm	
11pm		11pm		11pm	
12pm		12pm		12pm	

Wheel of Life

To-do

Reflections

Notes

Quotations & Tips

POWERFUL WOMEN TODAY

Month [   ] Year [   ]

SUNDAY ⬤	MONDAY ⬤	TUESDAY ⬤	WEDNESDAY ⬤
6am	6am	6am	6am
7am	7am	7am	7am
8am	8am	8am	8am
9am	9am	9am	9am
10am	10am	10am	10am
11am	11am	11am	11am
12pm	12pm	12pm	12pm
1pm	1pm	1pm	1pm
2pm	2pm	2pm	2pm
3pm	3pm	3pm	3pm
4pm	4pm	4pm	4pm
5pm	5pm	5pm	5pm
6pm	6pm	6pm	6pm
7pm	7pm	7pm	7pm
8pm	8pm	8pm	8pm
9pm	9pm	9pm	9pm
10pm	10pm	10pm	10pm
11pm	11pm	11pm	11pm
12pm	12pm	12pm	12pm

"When I believe in something, I'm like a dog with a bone."
— Melissa McCarthy

WEEKLY
CHECK INS

THURSDAY	⚪	FRIDAY	⚪	SATURDAY	⚪
6am		6am		6am	
7am		7am		7am	
8am		8am		8am	
9am		9am		9am	
10am		10am		10am	
11am		11am		11am	
12pm		12pm		12pm	
1pm		1pm		1pm	
2pm		2pm		2pm	
3pm		3pm		3pm	
4pm		4pm		4pm	
5pm		5pm		5pm	
6pm		6pm		6pm	
7pm		7pm		7pm	
8pm		8pm		8pm	
9pm		9pm		9pm	
10pm		10pm		10pm	
11pm		11pm		11pm	
12pm		12pm		12pm	

Wheel of Life

To-do

Reflections

Notes

Quotations & Tips

POWERFUL
WOMEN TODAY

Month			Year	

SUNDAY ●	MONDAY ●	TUESDAY ●	WEDNESDAY ●
6am	6am	6am	6am
7am	7am	7am	7am
8am	8am	8am	8am
9am	9am	9am	9am
10am	10am	10am	10am
11am	11am	11am	11am
12pm	12pm	12pm	12pm
1pm	1pm	1pm	1pm
2pm	2pm	2pm	2pm
3pm	3pm	3pm	3pm
4pm	4pm	4pm	4pm
5pm	5pm	5pm	5pm
6pm	6pm	6pm	6pm
7pm	7pm	7pm	7pm
8pm	8pm	8pm	8pm
9pm	9pm	9pm	9pm
10pm	10pm	10pm	10pm
11pm	11pm	11pm	11pm
12pm	12pm	12pm	12pm

"I need to listen well so that I hear what is not said."
— *Thuli Madonsela*

THURSDAY	⬤	FRIDAY	⬤	SATURDAY	⬤
6am		6am		6am	
7am		7am		7am	
8am		8am		8am	
9am		9am		9am	
10am		10am		10am	
11am		11am		11am	
12pm		12pm		12pm	
1pm		1pm		1pm	
2pm		2pm		2pm	
3pm		3pm		3pm	
4pm		4pm		4pm	
5pm		5pm		5pm	
6pm		6pm		6pm	
7pm		7pm		7pm	
8pm		8pm		8pm	
9pm		9pm		9pm	
10pm		10pm		10pm	
11pm		11pm		11pm	
12pm		12pm		12pm	

WEEKLY
CHECK INS

Wheel of Life

To-do

Reflections

Notes

Quotations & Tips

POWERFUL
WOMEN TODAY

Month _____ Year ____

SUNDAY ⬤	MONDAY ⬤	TUESDAY ⬤	WEDNESDAY ⬤
6am	6am	6am	6am
7am	7am	7am	7am
8am	8am	8am	8am
9am	9am	9am	9am
10am	10am	10am	10am
11am	11am	11am	11am
12pm	12pm	12pm	12pm
1pm	1pm	1pm	1pm
2pm	2pm	2pm	2pm
3pm	3pm	3pm	3pm
4pm	4pm	4pm	4pm
5pm	5pm	5pm	5pm
6pm	6pm	6pm	6pm
7pm	7pm	7pm	7pm
8pm	8pm	8pm	8pm
9pm	9pm	9pm	9pm
10pm	10pm	10pm	10pm
11pm	11pm	11pm	11pm
12pm	12pm	12pm	12pm

"It's not the absence of fear, it's overcoming it. Sometimes you've got to blast through and have faith." — *Emma Watson*

THURSDAY ⬤		FRIDAY ⬤		SATURDAY ⬤	
6am		6am		6am	
7am		7am		7am	
8am		8am		8am	
9am		9am		9am	
10am		10am		10am	
11am		11am		11am	
12pm		12pm		12pm	
1pm		1pm		1pm	
2pm		2pm		2pm	
3pm		3pm		3pm	
4pm		4pm		4pm	
5pm		5pm		5pm	
6pm		6pm		6pm	
7pm		7pm		7pm	
8pm		8pm		8pm	
9pm		9pm		9pm	
10pm		10pm		10pm	
11pm		11pm		11pm	
12pm		12pm		12pm	

WEEKLY
CHECK INS

Wheel of Life

To-do

Reflections

Notes

Quotations & Tips

POWERFUL
WOMEN TODAY

Month		Year	

SUNDAY ●	MONDAY ●	TUESDAY ●	WEDNESDAY ●
6am	6am	6am	6am
7am	7am	7am	7am
8am	8am	8am	8am
9am	9am	9am	9am
10am	10am	10am	10am
11am	11am	11am	11am
12pm	12pm	12pm	12pm
1pm	1pm	1pm	1pm
2pm	2pm	2pm	2pm
3pm	3pm	3pm	3pm
4pm	4pm	4pm	4pm
5pm	5pm	5pm	5pm
6pm	6pm	6pm	6pm
7pm	7pm	7pm	7pm
8pm	8pm	8pm	8pm
9pm	9pm	9pm	9pm
10pm	10pm	10pm	10pm
11pm	11pm	11pm	11pm
12pm	12pm	12pm	12pm

"And the day came when the risk to remain tight in a bud was more painful than the risk it took to blossom." — Anaïs Nin

THURSDAY	⚪	FRIDAY	⚪	SATURDAY	⚪
6am		6am		6am	
7am		7am		7am	
8am		8am		8am	
9am		9am		9am	
10am		10am		10am	
11am		11am		11am	
12pm		12pm		12pm	
1pm		1pm		1pm	
2pm		2pm		2pm	
3pm		3pm		3pm	
4pm		4pm		4pm	
5pm		5pm		5pm	
6pm		6pm		6pm	
7pm		7pm		7pm	
8pm		8pm		8pm	
9pm		9pm		9pm	
10pm		10pm		10pm	
11pm		11pm		11pm	
12pm		12pm		12pm	

Wheel of Life

To-do

Reflections

Notes

Quotations & Tips

POWERFUL WOMEN TODAY

Month		Year	

SUNDAY ●	MONDAY ●	TUESDAY ●	WEDNESDAY ●
6am	6am	6am	6am
7am	7am	7am	7am
8am	8am	8am	8am
9am	9am	9am	9am
10am	10am	10am	10am
11am	11am	11am	11am
12pm	12pm	12pm	12pm
1pm	1pm	1pm	1pm
2pm	2pm	2pm	2pm
3pm	3pm	3pm	3pm
4pm	4pm	4pm	4pm
5pm	5pm	5pm	5pm
6pm	6pm	6pm	6pm
7pm	7pm	7pm	7pm
8pm	8pm	8pm	8pm
9pm	9pm	9pm	9pm
10pm	10pm	10pm	10pm
11pm	11pm	11pm	11pm
12pm	12pm	12pm	12pm

"Don't live life in the past lane." — *Samantha Ettus*

THURSDAY	○	FRIDAY	○	SATURDAY	○
6am		6am		6am	
7am		7am		7am	
8am		8am		8am	
9am		9am		9am	
10am		10am		10am	
11am		11am		11am	
12pm		12pm		12pm	
1pm		1pm		1pm	
2pm		2pm		2pm	
3pm		3pm		3pm	
4pm		4pm		4pm	
5pm		5pm		5pm	
6pm		6pm		6pm	
7pm		7pm		7pm	
8pm		8pm		8pm	
9pm		9pm		9pm	
10pm		10pm		10pm	
11pm		11pm		11pm	
12pm		12pm		12pm	

WEEKLY
CHECK INS

Wheel of Life

To-do

Reflections

Notes

Quotations & Tips

POWERFUL
WOMEN TODAY

Month			Year	

SUNDAY	●	MONDAY	●	TUESDAY	●	WEDNESDAY	●
6am		6am		6am		6am	
7am		7am		7am		7am	
8am		8am		8am		8am	
9am		9am		9am		9am	
10am		10am		10am		10am	
11am		11am		11am		11am	
12pm		12pm		12pm		12pm	
1pm		1pm		1pm		1pm	
2pm		2pm		2pm		2pm	
3pm		3pm		3pm		3pm	
4pm		4pm		4pm		4pm	
5pm		5pm		5pm		5pm	
6pm		6pm		6pm		6pm	
7pm		7pm		7pm		7pm	
8pm		8pm		8pm		8pm	
9pm		9pm		9pm		9pm	
10pm		10pm		10pm		10pm	
11pm		11pm		11pm		11pm	
12pm		12pm		12pm		12pm	

"Many receive advice, only the wise profit from it."
— Harper Lee

WEEKLY
CHECK INS

THURSDAY	⬤	FRIDAY	⬤	SATURDAY	⬤
6am		6am		6am	
7am		7am		7am	
8am		8am		8am	
9am		9am		9am	
10am		10am		10am	
11am		11am		11am	
12pm		12pm		12pm	
1pm		1pm		1pm	
2pm		2pm		2pm	
3pm		3pm		3pm	
4pm		4pm		4pm	
5pm		5pm		5pm	
6pm		6pm		6pm	
7pm		7pm		7pm	
8pm		8pm		8pm	
9pm		9pm		9pm	
10pm		10pm		10pm	
11pm		11pm		11pm	
12pm		12pm		12pm	

Wheel of Life

To-do

Reflections

Notes

Quotations & Tips

POWERFUL
WOMEN TODAY

HOLIDAY	2022			2023			2024		
New Year's Day	Jan	Saturday	1	Jan	Sunday	1	Jan	Monday	1
Martin Luther King Jr. Day	Jan	Monday	17	Jan	Monday	16	Jan	Monday	15
Groundhog Day	Feb	Wednesday	2	Feb	Thursday	2	Feb	Friday	2
Lincoln's Birthday	Feb	Saturday	12	Feb	Sunday	12	Feb	Monday	12
St. Valentine's Day	Feb	Monday	14	Feb	Tuesday	14	Feb	Wednesday	14
President's Day	Feb	Monday	21	Feb	Monday	20	Feb	Monday	19
Ash Wednesday	Mar	Wednesday	2	Feb	Wednesday	22	Feb	Wednesday	14
Washington's Birthday	Feb	Tuesday	22	Feb	Wednesday	22	Feb	Thursday	22
Orthodox Lent Begins	Mar	Monday	7	Feb	Monday	27	Mar	Monday	18
Daylight Saving Time Begins	Mar	Sunday	13	Mar	Sunday	12	Mar	Sunday	10
St. Patrick's Day	Mar	Thursday	17	Mar	Friday	17	Mar	Sunday	17
First Day of Spring	Mar	Sunday	20	Mar	Monday	20	Mar	Wednesday	20
Palm Sunday	Apr	Sunday	10	Apr	Sunday	2	Mar	Sunday	24
April Fool's Day	Apr	Friday	1	Apr	Saturday	1	Apr	Monday	1
Good Friday	Apr	Friday	15	Apr	Friday	7	Mar	Friday	29
Passover*	Apr	Friday	15	Apr	Wednesday	5	Apr	Tuesday	23
Easter Sunday	Apr	Sunday	17	Apr	Sunday	9	Mar	Sunday	31
Eastery Monday (CAN)	Apr	Monday	18	Apr	Monday	10	Arp	Monday	1
Orthodox Easter (Pascha)	Apr	Sunday	24	Apr	Sunday	16	May	Sunday	5
Earth Day	Apr	Friday	22	Apr	Saturday	22	Apr	Monday	22
Administrative Professional Day	Apr	Wednesday	27	Apr	Wednesday	26	Apr	Wednesday	24
Arbor Day	Apr	Friday	29	Apr	Friday	28	Apr	Friday	26
Mother's Day	May	Sunday	8	May	Sunday	14	May	Sunday	12
Armed Forces Day	May	Saturday	21	May	Saturday	20	May	Saturday	18
Victoria Day (CAN)	May	Monday	23	May	Monday	22	May	Monday	20
Memorial Day Observed	May	Monday	30	May	Monday	29	May	Monday	27
Flag Day	Jun	Tuesday	14	Jun	Wednesday	14	Jun	Friday	14
Father's Day	Jun	Sunday	19	Jun	Sunday	18	Jun	Sunday	16
First Day of Summer	Jun	Tuesday	21	Jun	Wednesday	21	Jun	Friday	21
Canada Day (CAN)	Jul	Friday	1	Jul	Saturday	1	Jul	Monday	1
Independence Day	Jul	Monday	4	Jul	Tuesday	4	Jul	Thursday	4
Civic Day (CAN)	Aug	Monday	1	Aug	Monday	7	Aug	Monday	5
Labor Day	Sep	Sunday	5	Sep	Monday	4	Sep	Monday	2
Grandparent's Day	Sep	Sunday	11	Sep	Sunday	10	Sep	Sunday	8
Patriot Day	Sep	Sunday	11	Sep	Monday	11	Sep	Wednesday	11
Rosh Hashanah*	Sep	Saturday	25	Sep	Friday	15	Oct	Thursday	3
Citizenship Day	Sep	Thursday	17	Sep	Sunday	17	Sep	Tuesday	17
First Day of Autumn	Sep	Tuesday	22	Sep	Saturday	23	Sep	Sunday	22
Yom Kippur*	Oct	Monday	4	Sep	Sunday	24	Oct	Saturday	12
Columbus Day Observed	Oct	Monday	10	Oct	Monday	9	Oct	Monday	14
Thanksgiving Day (CAN)	Oct	Saturday	10	Oct	Monday	9	Oct	Monday	14
Sweetest Day	Oct	Tuesday	15	Oct	Saturday	21	Oct	Saturday	19
United Nations Day	Oct	Monday	24	Oct	Tuesday	24	Oct	Thursday	24
Halloween	Oct	Monday	31	Oct	Tuesday	31	Oct	Thursday	31
Daylight Saving Time Ends	Nov	Sunday	6	Nov	Sunday	5	Nov	Sunday	3
Election Day	Nov	Tuesday	8	Nov	Tuesday	7	Nov	Tuesday	5
Veterans Day	Nov	Friday	11	Nov	Saturday	11	Nov	Monday	11
Remembrance Day (CAN)	Nov	Friday	11	Nov	Saturday	11	Nov	Monday	11
Thanksgiving Day	Nov	Thursday	24	Nov	Thursday	23	Nov	Thursday	28
Pearl Harbor Day	Dec	Wednesday	7	Dec	Thursday	7	Dec	Saturday	7
Hanukkah*	Dec	Sunday	18	Dec	Thursday	7	Dec	Thursday	26
First Day of Winter	Dec	Wednesday	21	Dec	Thursday	21	Dec	Saturday	21
Christmas Day	Dec	Sunday	25	Dec	Monday	25	Dec	Wednesday	25
Boxing Day (CAN)	Dec	Monday	26	Dec	Tuesday	26	Dec	Thursday	26
New Year's Eve	Dec	Saturday	31	Dec	Sunday	31	Dec	Tuesday	31

2022

JANUARY
S	M	T	W	T	F	S
						1
2	3	4	5	6	7	8
9	10	11	12	13	14	15
16	17	18	19	20	21	22
23	24	25	26	27	28	29
30	31					

FEBRUARY
S	M	T	W	T	F	S
		1	2	3	4	5
6	7	8	9	10	11	12
13	14	15	16	17	18	19
20	21	22	23	24	25	26
27	28					

MARCH
S	M	T	W	T	F	S
		1	2	3	4	5
6	7	8	9	10	11	12
13	14	15	16	17	18	19
20	21	22	23	24	25	26
27	28	29	30	31		

APRIL
S	M	T	W	T	F	S
					1	2
3	4	5	6	7	8	9
10	11	12	13	14	15	16
17	18	19	20	21	22	23
24	25	26	27	28	29	30

MAY
S	M	T	W	T	F	S
1	2	3	4	5	6	7
8	9	10	11	12	13	14
15	16	17	18	19	20	21
22	23	24	25	26	27	28
29	30	31				

JUNE
S	M	T	W	T	F	S
			1	2	3	4
5	6	7	8	9	10	11
12	13	14	15	16	17	18
19	20	21	22	23	24	25
26	27	28	29	30		

JULY
S	M	T	W	T	F	S
					1	2
3	4	5	6	7	8	9
10	11	12	13	14	15	16
17	18	19	20	21	22	23
24	25	26	27	28	29	30
31						

AUGUST
S	M	T	W	T	F	S
	1	2	3	4	5	6
7	8	9	10	11	12	13
14	15	16	17	18	19	20
21	22	23	24	25	26	27
28	29	30	31			

SEPTEMBER
S	M	T	W	T	F	S
				1	2	3
4	5	6	7	8	9	10
11	12	13	14	15	16	17
18	19	20	21	22	23	24
25	26	27	28	29	30	

OCTOBER
S	M	T	W	T	F	S
						1
2	3	4	5	6	7	8
9	10	11	12	13	14	15
16	17	18	19	20	21	22
23	24	25	26	27	28	29
30	31					

NOVEMBER
S	M	T	W	T	F	S
		1	2	3	4	5
6	7	8	9	10	11	12
13	14	15	16	17	18	19
20	21	22	23	24	25	26
27	28	29	30			

DECEMBER
S	M	T	W	T	F	S
				1	2	3
4	5	6	7	8	9	10
11	12	13	14	15	16	17
18	19	20	21	22	23	24
25	26	27	28	29	30	31

2023

JANUARY
S	M	T	W	T	F	S
1	2	3	4	5	6	7
8	9	10	11	12	13	14
15	16	17	18	19	20	21
22	23	24	25	26	27	28
29	30	31				

FEBRUARY
S	M	T	W	T	F	S
			1	2	3	4
5	6	7	8	9	10	11
12	13	14	15	16	17	18
19	20	21	22	23	24	25
26	27	28				

MARCH
S	M	T	W	T	F	S
			1	2	3	4
5	6	7	8	9	10	11
12	13	14	15	16	17	18
19	20	21	22	23	24	25
26	27	28	29	30	31	

APRIL
S	M	T	W	T	F	S
						1
2	3	4	5	6	7	8
9	10	11	12	13	14	15
16	17	18	19	20	21	22
23	24	25	26	27	28	29
30						

MAY
S	M	T	W	T	F	S
	1	2	3	4	5	6
7	8	9	10	11	12	13
14	15	16	17	18	19	20
21	22	23	24	25	26	27
28	29	30	31			

JUNE
S	M	T	W	T	F	S
				1	2	3
4	5	6	7	8	9	10
11	12	13	14	15	16	17
18	19	20	21	22	23	24
25	26	27	28	29	30	

JULY
S	M	T	W	T	F	S
						1
2	3	4	5	6	7	8
9	10	11	12	13	14	15
16	17	18	19	20	21	22
23	24	25	26	27	28	29
30	31					

AUGUST
S	M	T	W	T	F	S
		1	2	3	4	5
6	7	8	9	10	11	12
13	14	15	16	17	18	19
20	21	22	23	24	25	26
27	28	29	30	31		

SEPTEMBER
S	M	T	W	T	F	S
					1	2
3	4	5	6	7	8	9
10	11	12	13	14	15	16
17	18	19	20	21	22	23
24	25	26	27	28	29	30

OCTOBER
S	M	T	W	T	F	S
1	2	3	4	5	6	7
8	9	10	11	12	13	14
15	16	17	18	19	20	21
22	23	24	25	26	27	28
29	30	31				

NOVEMBER
S	M	T	W	T	F	S
			1	2	3	4
5	6	7	8	9	10	11
12	13	14	15	16	17	18
19	20	21	22	23	24	25
26	27	28	29	30		

DECEMBER
S	M	T	W	T	F	S
					1	2
3	4	5	6	7	8	9
10	11	12	13	14	15	16
17	18	19	20	21	22	23
24	25	26	27	28	29	30
31						

2024

JANUARY
S	M	T	W	T	F	S
	1	2	3	4	5	6
7	8	9	10	11	12	13
14	15	16	17	18	19	20
21	22	23	24	25	26	27
28	29	30	31			

FEBRUARY
S	M	T	W	T	F	S
				1	2	3
4	5	6	7	8	9	10
11	12	13	14	15	16	17
18	19	20	21	22	23	24
25	26	27	28	29		

MARCH
S	M	T	W	T	F	S
					1	2
3	4	5	6	7	8	9
10	11	12	13	14	15	16
17	18	19	20	21	22	23
24	25	26	27	28	29	30
31						

APRIL
S	M	T	W	T	F	S
	1	2	3	4	5	6
7	8	9	10	11	12	13
14	15	16	17	18	19	20
21	22	23	24	25	26	27
28	29	30				

MAY
S	M	T	W	T	F	S
			1	2	3	4
5	6	7	8	9	10	11
12	13	14	15	16	17	18
19	20	21	22	23	24	25
26	27	28	29	30	31	

JUNE
S	M	T	W	T	F	S
						1
2	3	4	5	6	7	8
9	10	11	12	13	14	15
16	17	18	19	20	21	22
23	24	25	26	27	28	29
30						

JULY
S	M	T	W	T	F	S
	1	2	3	4	5	6
7	8	9	10	11	12	13
14	15	16	17	18	19	20
21	22	23	24	25	26	27
28	29	30	31			

AUGUST
S	M	T	W	T	F	S
				1	2	3
4	5	6	7	8	9	10
11	12	13	14	15	16	17
18	19	20	21	22	23	24
25	26	27	28	29	30	31

SEPTEMBER
S	M	T	W	T	F	S
1	2	3	4	5	6	7
8	9	10	11	12	13	14
15	16	17	18	19	20	21
22	23	24	25	26	27	28
29	30					

OCTOBER
S	M	T	W	T	F	S
		1	2	3	4	5
6	7	8	9	10	11	12
13	14	15	16	17	18	19
20	21	22	23	24	25	26
27	28	29	30	31		

NOVEMBER
S	M	T	W	T	F	S
					1	2
3	4	5	6	7	8	9
10	11	12	13	14	15	16
17	18	19	20	21	22	23
24	25	26	27	28	29	30

DECEMBER
S	M	T	W	T	F	S
1	2	3	4	5	6	7
8	9	10	11	12	13	14
15	16	17	18	19	20	21
22	23	24	25	26	27	28
29	30	31				

www.ingramcontent.com/pod-product-compliance
Lightning Source LLC
Chambersburg PA
CBHW042355030426
42336CB00030B/3491